Victorian Times

Jo Lawrie & Paul Noble

CollinsEducational
An imprint of HarperCollins*Publishers*
SKILLS AND RESOURCES SERIES

Published in 1991 by
CollinsEducational
An imprint of HarperCollins*Publishers*
77–85 Fulham Palace Road
Hammersmith
London W6 8JB

First published in 1990 by Unwin Hyman Ltd.

British Library Cataloguing in Publication Data

Noble, Paul, 1942–
Victorian times. – (Unwin Hyman Skills and resources series)
1. Great Britain
I. Title II. Lawrie, Jo
941.081

ISBN 0–00–312532–7

Cover photograph by Martin Chillmaid
Designed by Peter and Alex Tucker
Illustrated by Edward Ripley (Linda Rogers Associates)
Typeset by Acūté Design Consultants, Stroud, Glos
Printed in Great Britain by The Alden Press Limited, Oxford
Bound by Hunter & Foulis Limited

Acknowledgements

The authors and publishers would like to thank the following for permission to use photographs and documents:

Aerofilms (Mills Collection) 30
Ann Ronan Picture Library 12(tl), 12(br), 13(bl), 13(br), 65, 73, 86(t), 93(bl)
The British Architectural Library, RIBA, London 78
The British Museum 24, 75
HMSO 83, 84, 86(bl and r), 87
Hulton-Deutsch Collection 13(tl), 14(r), 15, 43, 46
The Illustrated London News Picture Library 32
India Office Library (British Library) 18
Chris Kington 81
London Museum 33
The Mansell Collection Limited 12(bl), 35(x2), 52, 54, 85
Mary Evans Picture Library 12(tr), 42
Mirror Features 58
Patrick Moyle 82(l)
National Portrait Gallery, London (A. Penley) 14(l)
Paul Noble 25, 59, 66
Mrs J Pearce 10
Post Office 13(tr), 90, 93(cl) (copyright reserved)
Public Record Office 26
Royal Victoria Infirmary, Newcastle-upon-Tyne 82(r)
St. Albans Museum 68
Reproduced by permission of the Trustees of the Science Museum 93(tl)
Wiltshire Record Office 20, 34, 55, 62, 63, 64, 76

We would like to give special thanks to the Wiltshire Record Office, whose help in arranging the supply of negatives has been much appreciated.

The publishers have made every effort to trace copyright holders, but if they have inadvertently overlooked any, they will be pleased to make the necessary arrangements.

Contents

Introduction

THE legacies of the Victorian age are all around us, both in our buildings and in our institutions. Early schools, the development of the railways, and indeed Queen Victoria herself, never fail to fascinate; these are topics that are popular with teachers and pupils alike.

The National Curriculum recognises the potential of this period, and nineteenth century themes continue to play an important role in primary history teaching. Many ideas relevant to the skills required in the National Curriculum documents are enclosed in this resource book; they have all been tried and tested in the classroom over many years.

'History is a splendid subject for study at any age but particularly so in school. Children are by nature curious and the past provides a feast for that curiosity.'

1.1 *The Final Report*, HMSO 1990

It is through their own investigations and discussions that children really begin to comprehend the links between past and present, and to enjoy the process of learning history. The activities in this book will help pupils to meet the attainment targets and to sustain the 'rigorous historical method' required. They will also allow pupils to take an active role and to acquire knowledge and understanding through first-hand experience.

National Curriculum History

For quick reference, we have listed below the attainment targets and the 'essential information' for CSU 3 of the Final Report; and for the latter we have identified the units in the book which you will find most relevant. However you will almost certainly want to make your own links and to use the themes in this book to meet your own teaching requirements.

The Attainment Targets

AT1: Knowledge and understanding of history
AT2: Interpretations of history
AT3: The use of historical sources

'Essential information' for CSU3

Final Report.	Units in this book
Queen Victoria, as national symbol	1A, 1D, 1E
Government and social reform	3I–K, 6A–C, 9A–F, 12C
Industry	3I, 6A, 6B, 12C, 15C
Transport	16A, 17B
Inventions and scientific discoveries	1F, 5A, 5B, 15C, 18A
Exploration	2A–C
Towns and cities	3A–E
Housing and health	3F–L, 4A–C, 6C
Population movements	8A, 8B
Importance of religion	13A, 19A, 19B
Architecture, art and literature	12A, 12B, 13A, 14A, 14B, 15A, 15B, 17A
Leisure and pastimes	10A, 10B, 11A–C

The book can also be used for Supplementary Study Units in Key Stage 2. Units in the book are also relevant to CSU 1, Key Stage 1, and some school designed local history units.

How to use this book

This photocopiable book has been divided into teacher's notes and pupil's pages.

The teacher's notes give background information on the theme and suggest ways in which you can use the pupil's pages. They also provide extension work and further ideas. These pages are designed to guide, inspire and, perhaps above all, save time. You will almost certainly want to add your own ideas for activities as you go through.

The pupil's pages are designed to be photocopied and contain a wide range of historical sources so that the children can carry out their own investigations. Some of the documents are a little difficult but, in our experience, children love to have an original document in front of them and to analyse and interpret the old handwriting. We have tried to make most of the work accessible to most children, but teachers should select and adapt activities where the abilities of the children so dictate.

The book is designed as a flexible resource. In some units there are a large number of pupil's pages and you may want to use each page separately, or, as in the case of pages 33 and 55 ('Punishment' and 'Transportation') use them for comparison. You may also want to enlarge some of the pupil's pages on the photocopier so that the lettering on some of the sources becomes larger and more readable.

History and everything else. How does it fit in?

Although the National Curriculum gives a prescription for primary history, it does not say how to teach it or how to fit it in with all the other subjects. This is for schools to decide. The strategy given below is intended to help you to find solutions that suit your school, your style of teaching, and your children.

1 Map your pathway through the National Curriculum. Choose the *content* (where there are choices to be made); the *focus* of school designed units; and the *order* in which the work is to be taught.

2 Examine your history curriculum for *links*. (A school designed unit on 'Victorian Children' could be fitted into a project on 'Victorian Britain', for example.) Running projects together like this could save valuable curriculum time, but it is better to run whole units together than to select isolated items from a number of units. Apart from breaking up the coherence of the course, you will end up with lots of isolated content that needs to be covered yet does not fit together.

3 Look for *links* that are *cross-curricular*. Again it might be better to look for opportunities for amalgamating whole science, technology or geography topics with history rather than picking out isolated elements.

4 The search for *cross-curricular links* need not, of course, start with history. It is preferable that one subject is chosen as the *lead* subject in a topic (see HMI report *Aspects of Primary Education: History and Geography*) which will mean that you must choose which content will be given more and which given less emphasis. There is no need to deal with all the prescribed content in equal measure.

There are other ways of approaching curriculum planning, for example through linking attainment targets, but whichever way you choose there are difficulties. Although the *statements of attainment* (at KS2 fewer than any other subject) contain some interesting guidance on what children should actually be able to do in history, one should avoid teaching to them, as this would be little different from teaching to a test. It is also easy to get hung up on content and forget the valuable processes and learning experiences that should be part of the curriculum.

This book provides a valuable resource and helpful suggestions on the use of IT, drama, evidence, art, craft, and a range of 'hands-on' experiences.

Going further with history

'Victorian Times' is for use in the classroom. However, we hope that the ideas presented here will inspire you – if you are not already inspired – to go out into your locality, or even further afield, to investigate the legacies of the Victorian age. Reference is made in the teacher's notes to places that you may want to go to, or archive work that you may be able to carry out, and the 'Useful Lists' section may help you to organise work or trips connected with Victorian times.

Enjoying history

All of these resources and activities have proved very successful in our schools and we hope that they will delight your children as they have ours.

Useful lists

Places to visit

The value of a visit decreases in proportion to the distance travelled so, generally speaking, close is best. It would therefore be inappropriate, not to say impossible, to print a comprehensive list of useful places. Specialist museums have been quoted in the text where appropriate (see, for example, Tiles and Childhood), so the following are merely sample lists.

For houses, period rooms or streets

Castle Museum, York
Geffrye Museum, London E2
The Museum of London, London EC2
Osborne House,* Isle of Wight
Royalty and Empire Exhibition, Windsor Station
Swindon Railway Cottages
Weald and Downland Open Air Museum, Singleton, Chichester

Victorian buildings (architect given)

Charles Barry: Houses of Parliament; Halifax Town Hall
Cuthbert Broderick: Leeds Town Hall; Grand Hotel Scarborough
William Butterfield: Keble College, Oxford; Exeter Grammar School
Charles Cockerell: Ashmolean, Oxford; St George's Hall, Liverpool
Augustus Pugin: St Chad's Cathedral, Birmingham; Scarisbrick Hall, Lancs
George Scott: Government Offices, Whitehall; Albert Memorial; Reading Gaol; Glasgow University

© *Industrial and other useful museums*
Armley Mill, Leeds
Bath Postal Museum
Beamish Open Air Museum, Durham
Black Country Industrial Museum, Dudley
Ironbridge Gorge Museum, Telford
Museum of English Rural Life, Reading
Museum of Science and Industry, Birmingham
National Museum of Photography and Film, Bradford
Pennine Farm Museum, Ripponden
Railway Museum, York

Displays of paintings, furniture and objects

These can be found in all major galleries but see particularly:
Abbey House Museum, Leeds
Art Gallery and Museum, Cheltenham
Bowes Museum, Barnard Castle
Cecil Higgins Art Gallery, Bedford
Ceredigion Museum, Aberystwyth
Grindon Museum, Sunderland
Victoria and Albert Museum, London

* Slides and books on Osborne House can be obtained from English Heritage, Postal Sales, PO Box 43, Ruislip

Historical fiction

Children's tastes and abilities vary enormously, so you will need to check whether a book is suitable for your particular children. A large number were written on this period during the 1950s and 1960s, many being set in the early part of the century. (Some of these books are now OP, out of print, but they should be available from good libraries.)

G. Avery *Ellen's Birthday*, Hamish Hamilton (OP)
Ellen and the Queen, Collins (OP)
The Call of the Valley, J. Goodchild 1986
W. Charles *The Lady from Scutari*, Blackie (OP)
G. Cross *The Iron Way*, OUP 1979
M. Darke *Ride the Iron Horse*, Kestrel (OP)
H. Graham *Shiva's Pearls*, Beaver (OP)
M. Lowett *Jonathan*, Faber (OP)
B. Mooney *The Stove Haunting*, Methuen 1986
E. Nesbit *The Railway Children*, Armada Books 1978
P. Pearce *Tom's Midnight Garden*,Penguin 1976
B. Willard *Jubilee*, Heinemann (OP)

Queen Victoria

WHERE better to begin a project on the Victorians than with Victoria? A statue of the queen may actually be in your locality. With luck, you may also have a Victoria Road, Hospital or Park just around the corner or perhaps a Jubilee Terrace or Albert Square. You must certainly survey your area for Victorian clues. Alternatively, you can examine a street map of London with the same object in mind. Victoria Station and the Victoria Line can make a neat link to the line of succession from Victoria to Elizabeth.

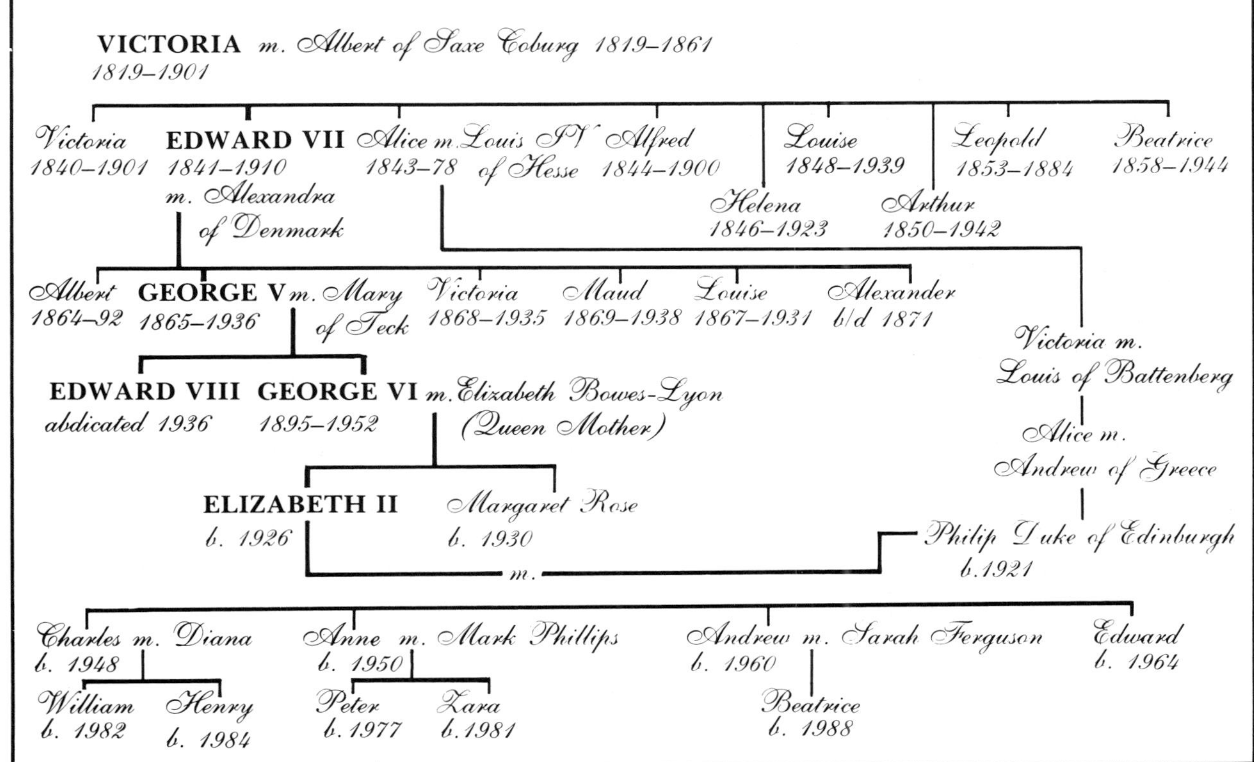

THIS family tree can be adapted to emphasise the line of succession. Name links – people with the same name (e.g. Beatrice) – are fascinating and can start children on a search for their own Victorian ancestors. Who were they? What were their names? What evidence can we find that they existed? A display entitled 'My Ancestors Were Victorians' could be fun. Ethnic minority children may add a valuable perspective here.

Sequencing and timelines

Children should physically arrange the events for the timeline (sheet 1A). This is to familiarise them with the content (and should be used for sheet 1F). The events for another, longer timeline could be illustrated. As sequencing comes before work with dates, children should be given the opportunity to do this with everyday objects, such as clothes pegs or school books. Indeed, sequencing can be done with almost anything!

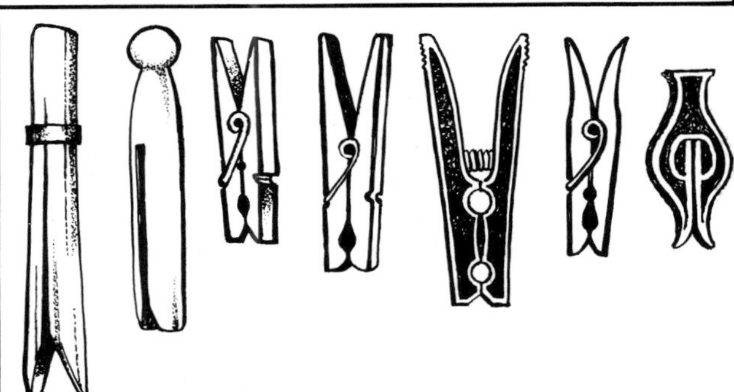

Children should first be introduced to personal timelines. Timelines should become a fixture of the classroom, to be added to and played with. An excellent timeline can be made by using a washing line and attaching pictures with clothes pegs. It can be used to pose challenges. Let children arrange illustrations of undated events in the correct time order. Dated markers can be left at fixed points, e.g. Queen Victoria's Jubilee, or death.

Sheets 1B and 1C provide more timeline material, which could perhaps be used as a quiz at the end of the topic. The class might like to write their own version of Walter Savage Landor's poem, to catalogue the achievements of the Victorian age. (For example, *I sing of Victoria, Queen/The finest ever seen . . .*)

> George the First was always reckoned
> Vile, but viler George the Second,
> And what mortal ever heard
> Any good of George the Third?
> When from earth the Fourth descended
> (God be praised!) the Georges ended.
>
> *Walter Savage Landor*

What was Victoria like?

Sheet 1D offers another starting-point for work on Victoria herself. Research for authentic detail to back up the diary extract will enable you to make a class frieze of the procession. Children will also delight in doing some of the things that Victoria did as a girl. Let them:

- Make a book using scallop shells for covers. (You should drill two holes through the shells for the retaining ribbons. If no shells are available, improvise by duplicating the shell drawn here and sticking it on card.) Stick the pages, drawn to size, on to card.
- Make a scrap book of Victorian pictures obtained from old greeting cards, etc. Victorian children liked to arrange facing pages symmetrically.
- Embroider a bookmark with their name. Plan the lettering on graph paper.
- Paint outdoor scenes or someone in Victorian dress, using water colours.

Jubilee celebrations

A number of schools took the opportunity to re-enact the Golden Jubilee celebrations of 1887 in the centenary year. No matter that it is past, your school can still have a successful event.

- Make Union Jacks, banners, and an archway decorated with greenery. (Flora Thompson's *Lark Rise to Candleford* contains memories of banner making.)
- Decorate 'commemorative' paper plates and cups out of cardboard, using photographs of the elderly Queen (sheet 1D).
- Dress up for a Jubilee tea-party in contemporary dress. Have real lemonade, lemon and barley water (see recipe), strawberry cordial, gingerbread, etc.
- Have a fair with stalls, sweets (sugar mice, aniseed balls, etc.), hurdy-gurdy man (use a hidden tape-recorder), Punch and Judy, Aunt Sally (stuff a 'head' with straw), human curiosities created by the children (four-armed people, very tall people, etc.), photographs of people's heads poked through a hole in a painted board (use a modern camera disguised as an old box camera on a stand).
- Learn the words and tune of the National Anthem to sing during the festivities.

Victorian Lemon and Barley Water

2 oz (55g) pearl barley
2 quarts (2.25l) of water
Thinly pared rind and juice of 2 lemons
Honey to taste

Wash the barley then place it in the water and bring it to the boil. Put the rind and juice of the lemons into a jug and pour on the boiling water with the barley. Stir in the honey to taste. Cover and leave to cool. Strain and serve.

Children and teachers re-enacting the Golden Jubilee celebrations of 1887

Victoria's life: a timeline

Here are some events to fit on a timeline for Queen Victoria. Cut them out and put them in the right place among these dates.

1810

1820

1830

1840

1850

1860

1870

1880

1890

1900

1910

Events in Queen Victoria's life

1840 Married Prince Albert

1861 Albert died, aged 41

1876 Became Empress of India

1901 Died, aged 81, at Osborne House, Isle of Wight.
Buried at Frogmore, Windsor

1837 Became Queen, aged 18

1819 Born in Kensington Palace, London

1887 Celebrated Golden Jubilee (50 years as Queen)

1897 Celebrated Diamond Jubilee

More facts about Queen Victoria

Queen Victoria was the longest reigning British monarch. She ruled for 63 years.

She had 9 children: 5 boys and 4 girls. Her youngest child, Beatrice, Princess of Battenberg, died in 1944.

Queen Victoria was related to most of the royal families of Europe.

Events: a picture quiz

Can you match the labels to the correct pictures?
Cut out the labels and the pictures and put them in time order.
Can you find out more details to write on the labels?

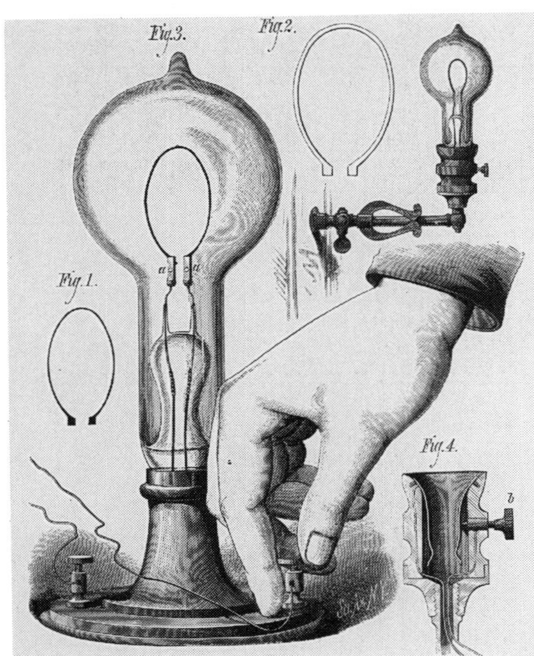

1879

1838

1885

1851

1851 Great Exhibition, London
1838 Fox Talbot invents positive/ negative photography
1885 First petrol-driven car built by Karl Benz (German)
1879 Edison makes the first light bulb

Events: a picture quiz

1863

1840

Black Sea

Turkey

1854

1825

1853

1840 Penny Post introduced

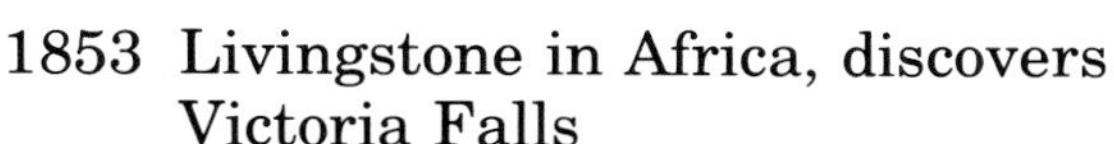

1853 Livingstone in Africa, discovers Victoria Falls

1854 Crimean War begins: Britain, France and Turkey against Russia

1863 World's first underground railway built in London

1825 Opening of the Stockton–Darlington railway, the first to carry passengers

Victoria: what was she like?

1D

We know what Victoria looked like because we have many pictures. Her diary gives us more clues to the sort of person she was.

What can we learn about Victoria from these pictures?
How did she change?

FACTFILE Height: 5 feet (1.52 metres), Hair: Fair, Eyes: Blue

Queen Victoria with great grandson, Edward VII.

The Golden Jubilee, 21 June 1887
This eventful day has come and is passed. The morning was beautiful and bright with fresh air. Troops began passing early with bands playing, and one heard constant cheering. Dressed, wearing a dress and bonnet, and pearls round my neck, with all my orders [badges of honour]. At half-past eleven we left the Palace, I driving in a handsomely gilt landau [golden carriage] drawn by six of the creams [horses of the same colour], with dear Vicky and Alix, who sat on the back seat. The crowds from the Palace gates up to the Abbey were enormous, and there was such an extraordinary outburst of enthusiasm as I had hardly ever seen in London before. I sat alone in the Abbey (oh! without my beloved husband, for whom this would have been such a proud day!) where I sat forty-nine years ago. The service was very well done. The 'Te Deum' [hymn], by my darling Albert, sounded beautiful.

From Queen Victoria's Diary

Victoria's famous silhouette

Silhouette portraits were popular in Victorian times. They were cheaper than photographs, which were a new invention.

Where might silhouettes like these be seen every day?

Can you guess how old the Queen was when they were drawn?

Cut out the silhouettes, mount them on card and frame them with silver foil to make them look Victorian.

Make your own silhouette. (Work with a friend.) Use a bright light from a desk lamp or a projector to cast your shadow on to a sheet of paper. Draw round the silhouette and cut it out for framing. You could make up a portrait gallery with some friends and try to guess who is who.

A family photograph

Why is Prince Albert missing from this photograph?
(The date will give you a clue. Look again at the timeline on sheet 1A.)

Large group photographs were only taken on special occasions. *Can you think what this one might be?*

Cut out or draw the people in the picture that you can name.

Queen Victoria's family in the 1870s

The Empire

EUROPEAN empires were part of the natural order in the nineteenth century. To the Victorians, Europe was the civilised world and so it was natural and inevitable that Europe should rule and civilise the rest. This was the 'white man's burden'. It has been calculated that, by 1845, 85 per cent of the earth's surface was in European hands. The European rush for empires actually occupied only about a quarter of the nineteenth century and acquiring an empire soon lost its attraction. In 1852 Disraeli expressed the conventional view when he said that 'the colonies are millstones round our neck'. Even so, Europeans seem to have been in no hurry to abandon their possessions and anti-colonialist reaction has been one of the major themes of twentieth-century history.

THE Empire is an area of study that is often neglected in primary schools, yet the concept of empire is an important one for children to understand. Imperialism is in present-day vocabulary. The British Empire was publicly a source of national pride until very recently and has left a visible mark upon Britain and its ex-colonies. The fact that English is widely spoken around the world is a legacy of its existence.

Children will perhaps have met the term 'empire' when studying the Romans or when watching films such as *The Empire Strikes Back*. These are good connections to make. Search for other empires. The Russian Empire and the Mongol Empire were two of the largest. With older children you could discuss whether or not empires are a 'good thing'.

Mapwork

Let the children come to grips with the sheer size of the British Empire (sheet 2A). Trace the development of some of the former colonies. Have they changed names? What marks have the days of the Empire left upon these countries? Why did the 'sun never set on the Empire'? (Let them look at a globe to answer this one.)

For the atlas work on sheet 2B the children should be aware that the Suez Canal was not opened until 1869.

Attitudes to the Empire

This extract from a Victorian schoolbook highlights the difficult question of attitudes.

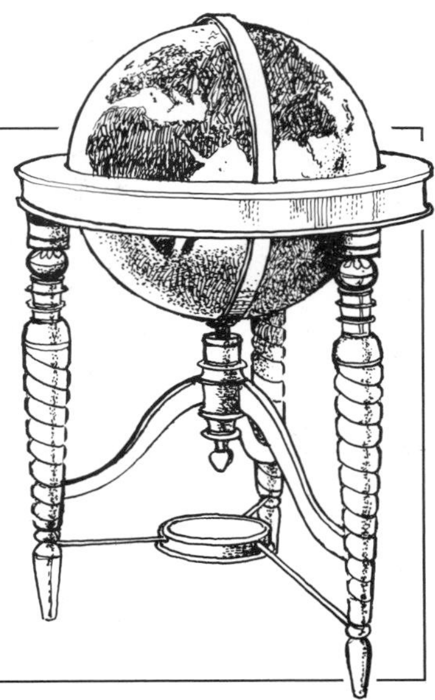

1. This is what we call 'Our Island Home'. It is one of the smallest and yet one of the most powerful nations in the world.
2. Our Queen rules over other parts of the world. The whole of her dominion is called the British Empire. It includes one-seventh part of the land surface of the globe.
3. London, the capital of England, is the largest and wealthiest city in the world.
4. Europe is the smallest of the continents but it is the most important. The countries of Europe are the homes of the chief nations of the Earth.
5. Most of these countries are inhabited by highly civilised people. Numerous manufactures are carried on in their great cities.

Why did the Victorians have this attitude to the rest of the world?

You may be able to arrange for the children to interview older adults for oral history. Plan the interviews carefully. What can they remember about the Empire?

Compile a broadcast entitled 'Memories of Empire'.

Examine the school log books (see page 56) for references to Empire Day celebrations. You may like to recreate them in some way.

Foreigners in a strange land

Sheet 2B could lead to an interesting project comparing India and the UK. Together with the newspaper cutting (sheet 2C), it provides a starting-point for discussion of what it is like to be a foreigner in an alien land. This may lead to interesting imaginative writing or links with other history projects. For example, how did the Normans feel when they settled in Britain? How do immigrants today feel? Introduce the word 'legacy'.

Consider also some of the things that India has given to Britain. For example, the idea for the Paisley design comes from India. We have absorbed a number of words from the Indian sub-continent into our language: bangle, bungalow, chintz, cot, doolally, loot, mango, pal, shampoo, etc. The BBC broadcast a series of programmes, *Plain Tales from the Raj*, full of wonderful background material; a book of the broadcast, with a useful index of Anglo-Indian, edited by Charles Allen, is now available (Futura).

A hunting party in India, 1870

A map of the British Empire

BRITISH POSSESSIONS IN VICTORIAN TIMES

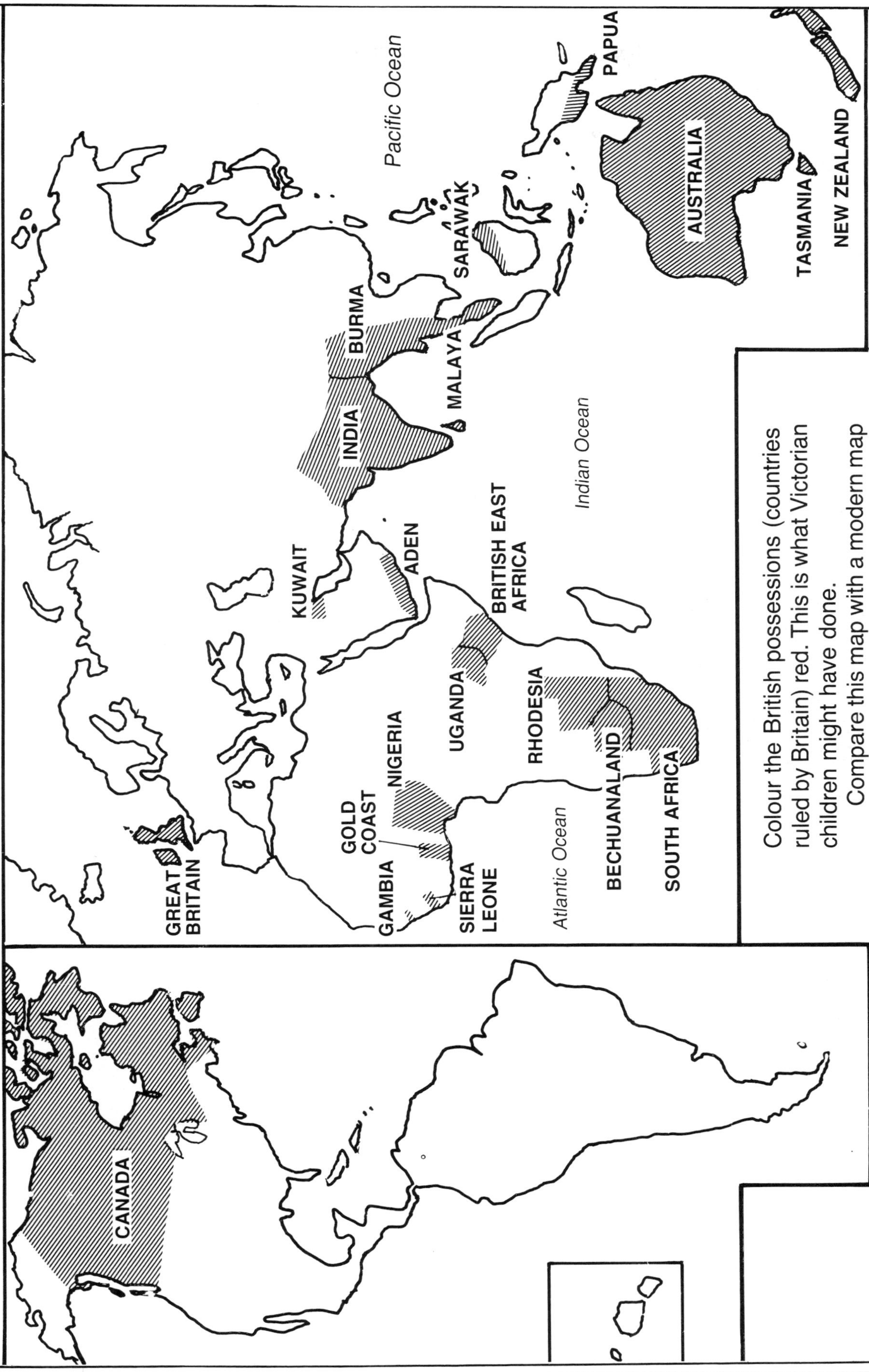

CANADA
GREAT BRITAIN
GAMBIA
GOLD COAST
NIGERIA
SIERRA LEONE
KUWAIT
ADEN
UGANDA
BRITISH EAST AFRICA
RHODESIA
BECHUANALAND
SOUTH AFRICA
INDIA
BURMA
MALAYA
SARAWAK
PAPUA
AUSTRALIA
TASMANIA
NEW ZEALAND
Atlantic Ocean
Indian Ocean
Pacific Ocean

Large areas of the world were ruled by the British during Queen Victoria's reign. People proudly boasted that 'the sun never sets on the Empire'.

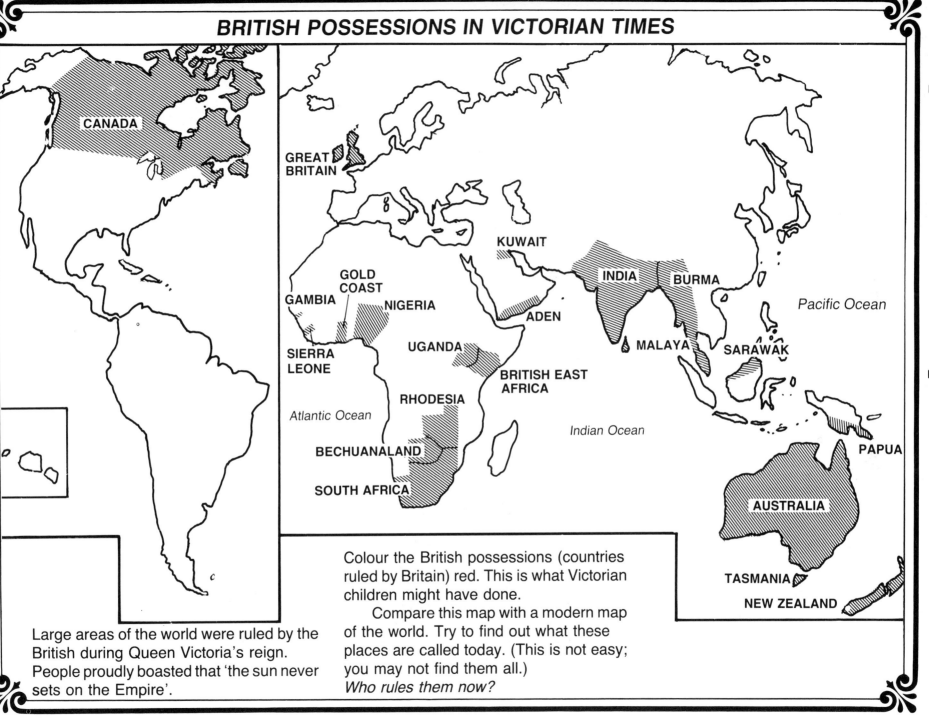

Colour the British possessions (countries ruled by Britain) red. This is what Victorian children might have done.

Compare this map with a modern map of the world. Try to find out what these places are called today. (This is not easy; you may not find them all.)

Who rules them now?

A tiger hunt in India

Here is part of the diary of a British officer who served in the army in India. He enjoyed India and took the trouble to learn the language. He also kept records of his main hobby. *What was that?*

Nownpoura

144 SATURDAY, MAY 19, 1860. (140—226.)

Started about 10a.m. 1st beat the ravine we
saw the bear in yesterday found nothing then
another very likely looking ~~place~~ ravine & then
another very long one, where I saw a tiger
sneaking under the opposite side (we were
on the top of a perpendicular part of the
ravine) I shot at him (missed). Diz made
a row about my having fired, as the
tiger was making off he fired 2 times at him
we then stationed ourselves lower down
in the ravine but to no purpose, coming
home the little Gray (Pig) fell as I was
going across the bed of a river, no grief in
consequence. I sent on my kit except
the bed to Mandlegurh about 8 p.m.
after I went to sleep on it came on to
rain I was awoke & went into Diz's tent.

HUNTING RECORD

1860 Month	Duck	Partridge	Black Do	Quail	Snipe	Rock Grouse	Hare	Shinkari	Black Buck	Bear	Bustard	F Florican
Brought over	49	3	-	45	53	1	2	4	1	1		
June 25th	-	-	-	-	-	-	-	-	2	-	-	1
— 28th	-	-	-	-	-	-	-	-	-	-	-	1
— 29th	-	-	-	-	-	-	-	1	-	-	-	
— 30th	-	-	-	-	-	-	-	-	-	1	2	
July 4th	-	-	-	-	-	-	-	-	1	3		
— 5th	-	-	-	-	-	-	-	-	4			
— 30th	-	-	-	-	-	-	-	-				
— 31st	-	-	-	-	-	-	-					

Handwriting is not always easy to read and historians often have to be very skilled to read evidence like this. Compare the original with the printed version below. *Do you think that the printed version is accurate?*

Started about 10 a.m. 1st [?] beat the ravine we saw the bear in yesterday found nothing then another very likely looking — ravine & then another very long one, where I saw a tiger sneaking under the opposite side (we were on the top of a perpendicular part of the ravine) I shot at him (missed). Diz [?] made a row about my having fired, as the tiger was making off he fired 2 times at him we then stationed ourselves lower down in the ravine but to no purpose, coming home the little Gray (Pig) fell as I was going across the bed of a river, no grief in consequence. I sent on my kit except the bed to Mandlegurh [?] about 8 p.m. after I went to sleep on it came on to rain I was awoke & went into Diz's [?] tent.

Use an atlas to trace the route that this officer took to India from Britain.
What differences would he have noticed in climate?
What else do you think he would have noticed?

The British Empire no longer exists but the Commonwealth is made up of some of the countries that used to be part of that Empire. Many people from the Commonwealth and their descendants now live in Britain.

Some British people stayed in India after India left the Empire and became independent. This newspaper report tells of some of them.

Fading remnants of the Raj who long for 'home'

Miss Porter and Mr Halpin are two survivors from a dwindling breed – Indian-born Britons who remained after the sub-continent gained its independence 40 years ago. None of the handful remaining in Lucknow has servants. They make do on pensions . . . that often amount to around £25 a month. Now many want to return to Britain but find the odds are against them.

Lucknow was once home to hundreds of Europeans . . . . The Britons who remain are descendants of shopkeepers or employees of the railways and post office. Miss Porter's father, Thomas, came to India with the army . . . and set up a shoe shop in Lucknow when he retired. She became a post office typist and retired as chief assistant to the postmaster.

'I live on one meal a day – I eat lunch and whatever is left over I have for tea.'

She is still sprightly, and is anxious to return to Britain – a country she has visited only once and that more than two decades ago. She has some relatives but they live in a council flat and have no room for her.

Henry Halpin was born in Bihar, where his father worked for the railways. He went to Britain in the 1930s and qualified as a chartered accountant.

He lives in a large, gloomy flat without running water. He is a cheerful man who divides his day between reading books from the British Council and worshipping every evening at the local Roman Catholic cathedral.

His larder rests on concrete stands which can be surrounded with water to deter insects and rodents; his few books are stored in plastic bags to keep out silverfish.

'I have really fond memories of my youth – you could go out with one anna (a sixteenth of a rupee) and buy a pocketful of toffees and things like that. However, independent India has not lived up to its expectations. There is nothing but trouble every day in this province.'

None of the Britons here can get used to the filthy conditions that prevail in north Indian cities and all speak with nostalgia of the cleanliness of English street life in the 1960s. As for other social changes since their last visits, they do not have much awareness or interest. None reads English newspapers or listens to the BBC World Service.

What was the 'Raj'?
How did these people come to be living in India?

Do you think that they feel British or Indian?
Give reasons for your opinions.

Population, poverty and crime 3

THE year of the first census was 1801, so nineteenth-century population figures have unprecedented reliability. Population growth is illustrated by the figures below.

	Population (millions)			
	England	Ireland	Scotland	Wales
1801	8.3	5.2	1.6	0.6
1831	13.1	7.8	2.8	0.9
1851	16.9	6.5	2.9	1.1

	Population		
	1871	1891	1901
Cardiff	40 000	129 000	165 200
Nottingham	87 000	214 000	240 400

London grew from 4 to 6.5 million in thirty years (1871-1901).

For most of the Victorian era, the infant mortality rate was around 150 per 1000 live births. In the 1860s, the average Victorian family had five or six children. However, family size steadily declined thereafter. Queen Victoria had nine children.

There was a shift in occupations into manufacturing trades although, as the census figures indicate (sheet 3D), there were local variations. At the midpoint of the century, one in four men still worked on the land, and more than a tenth of employed females were in domestic service.

Poverty is not always easy to define but it was certainly one of the major social problems of the period. Charles Booth (author of *Life and Labour of the People of London*, 1887) thought that the extent of poverty had been exaggerated until he carried out his own survey: between a quarter and a third of those he studied came within his own definition of poverty. Indirect evidence of poverty can be seen in the growth, during the last quarter of the century, of special charities such as the Poor Children's Boot Fund, the Country Holiday Society, and the Schools' Cheap Dinner Society. The workhouse (sheet 3I) was the last resort of the destitute. By the Poor Law Amendment Act (1834), parishes were grouped into unions which appointed guardians to administer workhouses. Once inside, families were separated and husbands and wives lived apart. It was a tough regime. There was a national scandal in 1840 when it was discovered that the inmates of the Andover workhouse were so hungry that they had gnawed at the bones that they were supposed to crush for fertiliser.

Population

OBTAIN some nineteenth-century census information from your local Record Office. It is often available on computer disks. (This is an excellent opportunity to cover the National Curriculum attainment targets relating to handling data on a computer.)*

Besides census returns, old school registers (if available) are a source of information on family size and on the popularity of first names at various times in the past (sheet 3A).

Faringdon Street (sheets 3B and C) can be represented on a large-scale frieze along a suitable corridor. Make the houses open-fronted and as large as possible and then all sorts of details can be added. There is scope for 'A day in the life of . . .' type of writing. Note that the census return is for 'New Swindon' – a new railway town built for the Great Western Railway. Workers came from all over the country.

There was a greater familiarity with both birth and death in Victorian homes than there is today. The pincushion (sheet 3E) is just one of the mementoes common in the period. You might encourage the children to look for more.

There were rigid rules about mourning, and funerals were often very elaborate and pompous. Victorian memorials in cemeteries are sometimes spectacularly grand. A study of gravestones links well with sheets 3A and 3F. Special mourning jewellery, memorial cards, and black-edged envelopes were produced. People even had brooches containing hair from the dead person. You may well come across some of this material during a project. Queen Victoria's excessive mourning for Albert had an impact on public life and came to be viewed with disfavour, in spite of the fact that over-attention to death was common.

* *A useful contact for this is the Norric Resource Centre, which produces the key census data handling package and programmes for handling graveyard data. These can be obtained from : The Norric Resource Centre, Coach Lane Campus, Newcastle-upon-Tyne. NE7 7AX.*

The workhouse

Try to track down the location of your local workhouse. (Use your County Record Office.) If it survives, what is it used for today? With help from your local Adviser, a drama day built around life in a workhouse could be attempted. The children will need lots of background information. Each child works out the role and life of an inmate: family details, job, reason for going to the workhouse. An adult plays the overseer, questioning the inmates about their reasons for becoming a 'burden on the parish'. The rules of the institution are read out, boring tasks are set. Males are separated from females. Medical examinations, workhouse clothes, bells for meals, gruel, prayers, and darkened rooms for sleep are features that might be considered.

Read the section about the workhouse from *Oliver Twist*. Enter into the spirit of the times and hold a soup kitchen in the playground on a cold day. Let the children make and eat gruel. Tell Dr Barnado's story.

The children will need background information on transportation for sheet 3J. This is covered in more detail in the section on emigrants (pages 52–3).

Alcoholism

Note that the 'wealth to poverty' cartoons (sheet 3L) are part of a series with a miserable ending. Gin was cheap and all alcoholic drinks dropped in price during Victorian times. Alcoholism was a major problem. The illustrator and caricaturist George Cruikshank (1792–1878) campaigned ingeniously against the excesses of drink. His cartoon 'The Bottle' sold over 100 000 copies in the first few days after publication (1847).

Alcoholism needs sensitive handling.

Gruel
1 tablespoon suet
1 teaspoon fine oatmeal
1 finely sliced onion
Pepper, salt, cinnamon to taste
Milk and/or water to give required consistency

Melt the suet and cook the onion in it until it is soft but not coloured. Add the seasoning and the oatmeal, stirring until the mixture binds to the spoon. Gradually add the liquid until it becomes a thick white sauce. This needs to be boiled well and thinned with more liquid as required. Serve piping hot.

Taking the census

A count, or 'census', of the population of Britain is taken every ten years. The first one was in 1801. *When will the next one be? Why are they needed?*

We can get some idea of which girls' and boys' names were popular from this cartoon. *What does it suggest about the size of Victorian families?*

Make two lists of the girls' and boys' names. Find out what are the most common names in your school today.

Are there any Victorian favourites? Old registers will help you to work out what were the most common names in the past.

Faringdon Street 1881

This is Faringdon Street. Use the census return sheet (3C) to find out who these people are. Name them and write down what you can find out about them.

Aged 62

NAME: ______________________

OCCUPATION: ______________________

PLACE OF BIRTH: ______________________

HOUSE NUMBER: ______________________

Aged 76

NAME: ______________________

OCCUPATION: ______________________

PLACE OF BIRTH: ______________________

HOUSE NUMBER: ______________________

Aged 37

NAME: ______________________

OCCUPATION: ______________________

PLACE OF BIRTH: ______________________

HOUSE NUMBER: ______________________

Census return sheet 1881

Page 30

The undermentioned Houses are situate within the Boundaries of the

~~Civil Parish~~ [~~or Township~~] of	~~City or Municipal Borough~~ of	~~Municipal Ward~~ of	Parliamentary Borough of	Town ~~or Village or Hamlet~~ of	Urban Sanitary District of	~~Rural Sanitary District~~ of	Ecclesiastical Parish or District of
Swindon			Cricklade	New Swindon	New Swindon		St Mark

No. of Schedule	ROAD, STREET, &c., and No. or NAME of HOUSE	HOUSES: Inhabited	HOUSES: Uninhabited (U.), or Building (B.)	NAME and Surname of each Person	RELATION to Head of Family	CONDITION as to Marriage	AGE last Birthday of: Males	AGE last Birthday of: Females	Rank, Profession, or OCCUPATION	WHERE BORN	(1) Deaf-and-Dumb (2) Blind (3) Imbecile or Idiot (4) Lunatic
127	12 Oxford St	1		Robert Drummond	Head	Mar	44		Foreman Engine Fitters	Scotland Kinbuck	
				Eliza do	wife	do		42		Do Saline Fifeshire	
				Margaret do	Dau	Unm		18	Pupil Teacher	Cheshire Crewe	
				William do	Son	do	17		App. Engine Fitter	do do	
				Eliza J. do	Dau			8	Scholar	Glam. London, Bridgend	
128	1 Faringdon St (North side)	1		Jane Heall	Head	W		67		Scotland Falkirk	
				James do	Son	Mar	28		Railz Engine Driver	Wilts Box	
				Kate do	Dau Law	do		24		Liverpool	
129	2 do	1		Robert Laxon	Head	Mar	46		Foreman Copper Smith	Norfolk Yarmouth	
				Maria do	wife	do		40		Bucks High Wycombe	
				Jane do	Dau	Unm		37	Tailoress	London	
				Maria do	do	Unm		35	Dress maker	do	
				Matilda do	do	do		26	do	Wilts Swindon	
				Amelia do	do	do		32	do	do do	
				Emma Keefe	Gd Dau	do		24	Tailoress	London	
130	3 do	1		William Laverick	Head	Mar	37		Forgeman	Northu. Bidlington	
				Maria do	wife	do		36		Dorset Weymouth	
				William R. do	Son		9		Scholar	Wilts Swindon	
				Muriel B. do	Dau			8	do	do do	
				James J. do	Son		6		do	do do	
				Fanny J. King	Serv	Unm		16	Gen. Serv	Mdx Kentish Town	
4	Total of Houses...	4			Total of Males and Females		7	14			

Census information

The information below came from census returns for the town of Prescot in Lancashire. These numbers tell all sorts of stories if you study them carefully.

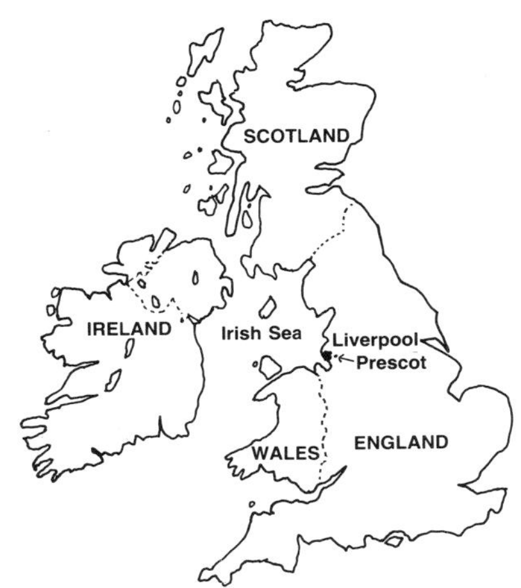

People living in Prescot

Where born	1851 Males	1851 Females	1871 Males	1871 Females
Prescot	1660	1679	1548	1524
Lancashire	519	596	500	460
Ireland	838	778	308	338
Elsewhere	164	159	203	196
Total:				
Males/females				
Population				

Males living in Prescot

Main occupations	1851	1861	1871
Bricklayer/labourer	49	30	36
Carter	25	28	16
Collier	139	44	57
Farm worker	315	149	85
General labourer	246	125	286
Pottery worker	37	8	9
School master	3	5	6
Shoe trade	73	52	37
Watchmaker and associated work	285	224	204

Females living in Prescot

Main occupations	1851	1861	1871
Charwoman	36	21	26
Coalminer	0	1	0
Dressmaker	45	33	31
Farm worker	67	30	20
Hawker	31	17	0
Housekeeper	32	24	25
Laundress/manglewoman	27	15	12
Nurse	18	11	15
Pedlar	27	0	1
Schoolmistress	11	9	14
Seamstress	18	2	3
Servant	211	168	181
Weaver	69	1	0

Can you answer these questions? (It may help to use a calculator.)

What was the total population in 1851 and in 1871?

Apart from Prescot itself, where were most people born in 1851?

Can you find out why they moved to Prescot?

Look at the three sets of figures for occupations.

What was the most common work for men?

What was the most common work for women?

What was the biggest change?

Perhaps you can make up some questions of your own.

Population growth

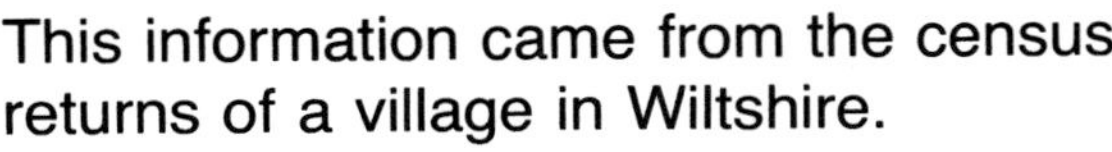

This information came from the census returns of a village in Wiltshire.

How many times bigger was this village in 1891 than in 1801?

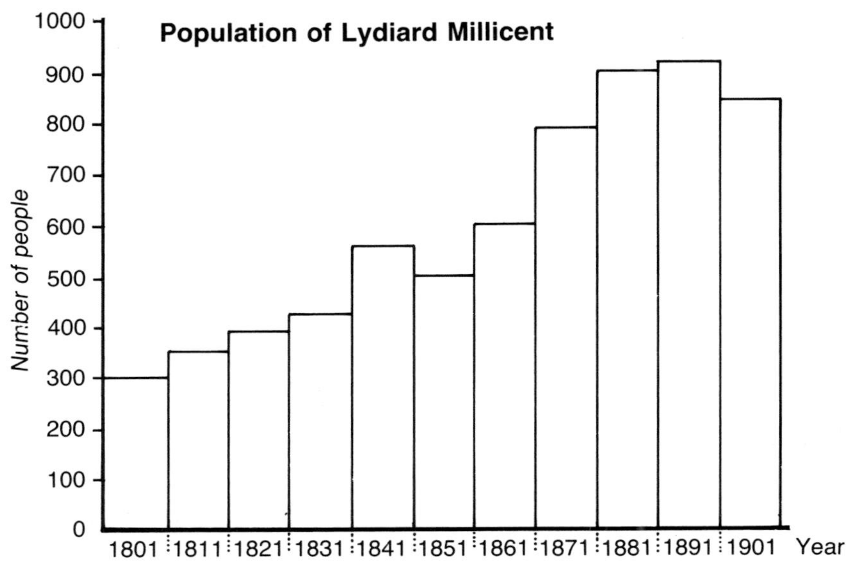

Families were large, so births were often being celebrated. This Victorian pincushion was specially made for this reason.

Did your mother keep a memento of your birth?

You can make a pincushion like this.
You will need:
Plain fabric 300 x 100 mm
Scissors
Needle and thread
Sawdust
Pins
Beads/sequins/ribbons/fringing for extra decoration

Cut out two pieces of fabric 150 x 100 mm. Pin them together with the right sides facing. Back-stitch around three sides, leaving one short side unstitched. Turn the right way out and press. Stuff with sawdust until plump. Turn in the edges and oversew the short side. Decorate with pins (make up your own saying). Add extra decoration as you wish.

Child deaths

These graphs show the numbers of child deaths in the village of Lydiard Millicent. Colour them.

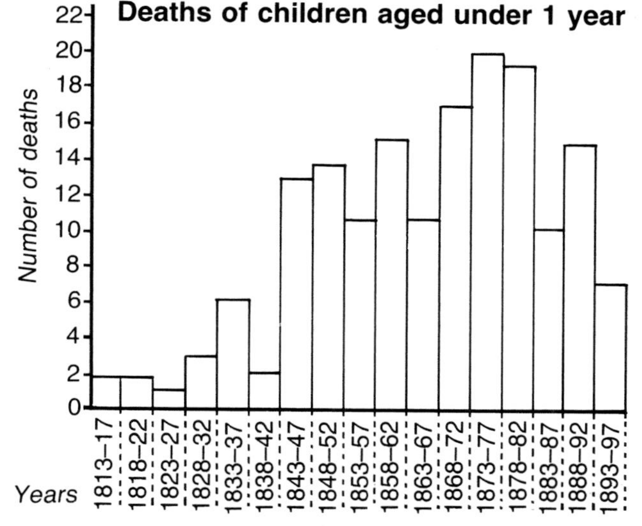

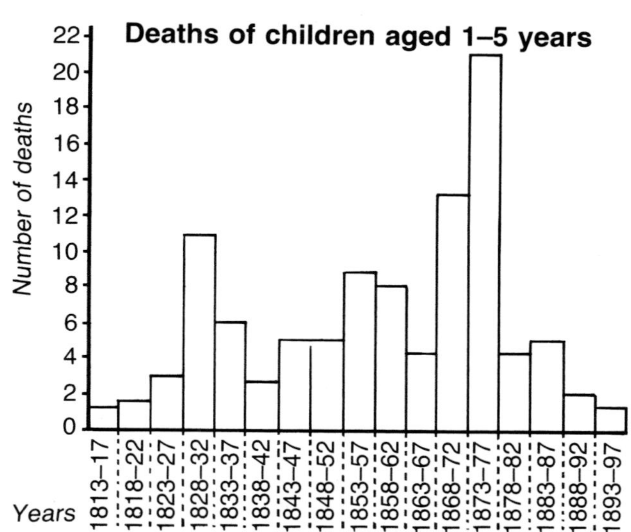

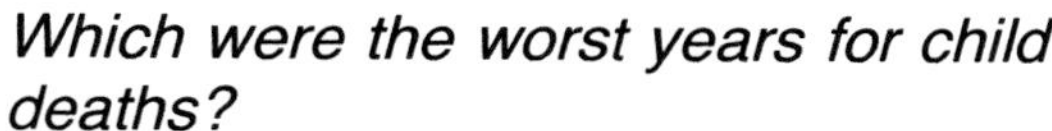

Which were the worst years for child deaths?

Make a graph showing *all* of the deaths for children under ten years old.

Can you explain what happened in the bad years?

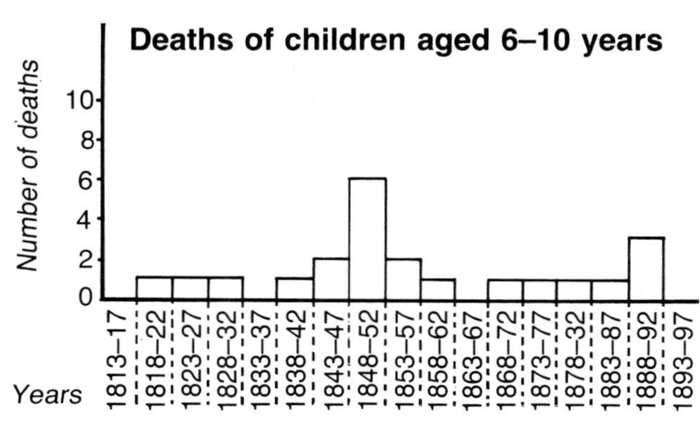

FACTFILE

1842: big increase in population after this date
1852-62: bad epidemic of smallpox
1848/1856/1879-80: very bad winters
1848-52/1858-62/1868-77: outbreaks of disease (especially scarlet fever and diphtheria)

Children of the poor

In the nineteenth century, Britain was one of the richest nations in the world, yet it had many poor people.

Can you tell the rich children from the poor children in this picture taken at the seaside? In how many ways do they differ?

Poor people had to send their children out to work in order to earn a little money. Try to find out what kinds of work children did in the big cities.

In the country, children worked in gangs on farms. Read the extract to find out what life was like for them.

Imagine that you are Harriet or Sarah (or else John or Amos). Write one page in your diary describing a day working in a gang. Explain how you felt during the day. Use the information here to help you to give a true picture.

In June 1862 my daughters Harriet and Sarah, aged . . . eleven and thirteen years, were engaged by a ganger to work on Mr Worman's land at Stilton. When they got there, he took them to near Peterborough; there they worked for six weeks, going and returning each day. The distance each way is eight miles [over 12 km], so that they had to walk sixteen miles each day on all the six working days of the week, besides working in the field from eight to five or half past five in the afternoon. They used to start from home at five in the morning, and seldom got back before nine. They worked at first on Mr Wyman's farm, close to the Peacock Inn, as you enter in for Peterborough, and afterwards they worked at Stanground. They had 7d. [3p] a day. They had to find all their own meals, as well as their own tools [such as hoes]. They [the girls] were good for nothing at the end of six weeks. They were very quick to work, and the ganger never gave them the stick.

Bad housing

Bad houses affected people's health, so, in 1884, a Royal Commission was set up to investigate the houses of the poor. One person who was questioned was a man called George Mitchell. This is what he said.

You were born in a house of two rooms, were you not?
Yes.
There were, I believe, father, mother, three girls and four boys all sleeping in the same room?
Yes.
Was this a fair sample of the other houses at the time?
It was.
I think you visited your village with a correspondent of *The Times*?
I did.
And you found there a room inhabited by 14 persons?
Yes.
In that room you found a father dying and a son dying in the same bed?
Yes.
Near the churchyard there was a house inhabited by 10 persons where there was no back door and the soil [sewage] of the closet was soaking through the wall of the house?
Yes, I saw it.
And you believe at this time there are 35-40 houses of the same kind in the village?
There are.

How does your house differ from George Mitchell's cottage?

Copy and fill in a chart like this. Use a full page.

Conditions	Where I live	Poor cottage in Victorian times
Heating		
Lighting		
Water		
Privacy		
Comfort		
Lavatory		
Number of people		
Rooms		

Dietary for able-bodied Men and Women

		BREAKFAST		DINNER				SUPPER	
		Bread	Boiled Milk with Oatmeal	Cooked Meat	Potatoes	Suet Pudding	Soup or Rice Milk	Bread	Boiled Milk with Oatmeal or Bread
		Ozs	Pints	Ozs	lbs	Ozs	Pints	Ozs	Pints
Sun ...	Men	6	1½	...	...	14	...	6	1½
	Women	6	1½	...	...	14	...	6	1½
Mon ...	Men	6	1½	5	½	...	...	6	1½
	Women	6	1½	5	½	...	...	6	1½
Tues ...	Men	6	1½	...	...	...	1½	6	1½
	Women	6	1½	...	...	...	1½	6	1½
Wed ...	Men	6	1½	...	...	14	...	6	1½
	Women	6	1½	...	...	14	...	6	1½
Thurs ...	Men	6	1½	...	...	...	1½	6	1½
	Women	6	1½	...	...	...	1½	6	1½
Fri ...	Men	6	1½	5	½	...	...	6	1½
	Women	6	1½	5	½	...	...	6	1½
Sat ...	Men	6	1½	...	...	...	1½	6	1½
	Women	6	1½	...	...	...	1½	6	1½

4 oz. of Bread to Soup and Rice Milk Dinners, to each Person.

Children under 9 years of age dieted at discretion. Sick dieted as ordered by the Medical Officer.

Old People above 60 years of age, may be allowed Tea, Coffee, Butter, and Sugar, (not exceeding 1 oz. of Tea, 2 oz. of Coffee, 3½ oz. of Butter, and 4 oz. of Sugar, per week each) in lieu of Gruel to Breakfast. Greens, occasionally, in lieu of Potatoes.

Marylebone workhouse dormitory, 1847

If you had no work, no money and nowhere to live, you might end up in a workhouse. Life in a workhouse was deliberately made hard.

What do these items tell you about life there?

Pretend that you have been put in a workhouse. Write a letter to a relative explaining how you 'fell on hard times' and ended up in the workhouse. Describe the conditions there and ask for help.

Plan of a workhouse

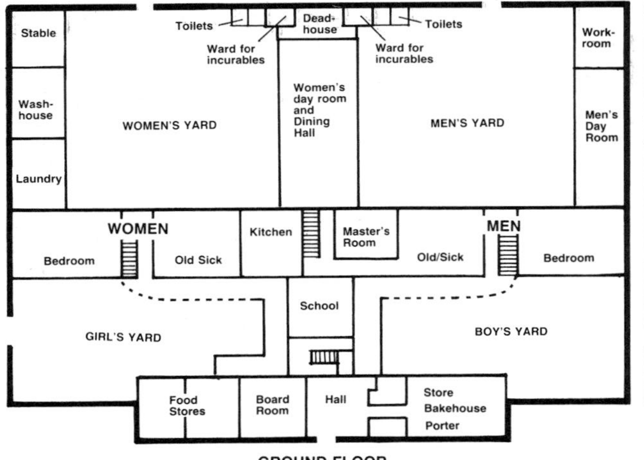

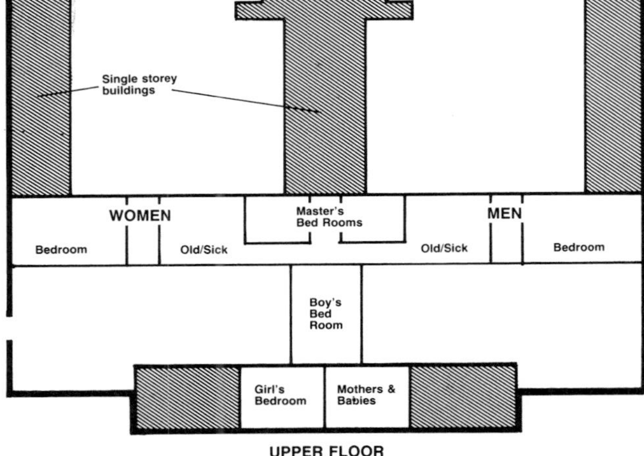

Punishment for criminals

What had these people done? Can you work out what happened to them? What else does this document tell us about them?

PRISONERS FOR TRIAL AT THE SESSIONS.

☞ The Prisoners marked (R. W. WELL,) read and write well. (R. W. IMP.,) read and write imperfectly. (R.,) read only. (N.,) neither read nor write. (SUP.,) superior.

County Gaol.

FELONY.

NO.		AGE.
1	ASHER WILLIAM RATTY, N.	21.
	To be confined in the new prison at Devizes for six months of hard labour	
2	GEORGE BRASHER. R.	19.
	To be transported for seven years and in the meantime to be confined in the County gaol —	
3	ELIZA JANE RANDALL. R. W. IMP.	19.
	To be confined in the County Gaol for six months of hard labour —	

Committed 3rd Jan. 1850, by H. Hetley, Esq. charged on the oaths of Elizabeth Bryant and others, with having feloniously stolen two Sheets, one Tablecloth, and other articles, the property of the said Elizabeth Bryant, at Netherhampton.

'Hard labour' sometimes meant hours on this. *What is it? What does it do?*

Can you think of a better punishment?

What might happen today?

Prison punishment book 1887

PRISONERS NAMES.	WHAT MISCONDUCT.	Date when committed 1887	WHAT PUNISHMENT.
Edward Cole	Talking	April 10	Dark Cell 24 hours
George Smith	Idleness	" 10	Bread & Water 2 days
John Howard	Defacing Wall	" 11	Dark Cell 26 hours
Louis Blackmore	Idleness	" 18	Ditto 24 hours
Wm Simmonds	Destroying Oakum	" 18	Ditto
John Frampton	Talking	" 20	Ditto
Edward Cole	Ditto	" 20	Ditto
William Hancock	Talking	" 24	Ditto
John Holcomb	Idleness	" 24	Ditto
Thomas Hamilton	Ditto	" 24	Bread & Water 2 days
William Jones	Ditto	" 25	Dark Cell 27 hours
John Farley	Ditto	" 25	Bread & Water 2 days
William Smith	Ditto	" 25	Dark Cell 48 hours
William North	Ditto	" 27	Bread & Water 3 days
Samuel Winslow	Destroying Oakum	May 2	Ditto 2 days
Edward Baker	Idleness	" 2	Ditto
William Morton	Destroying Oakum	" 2	Ditto
Solomon Gough	Idleness	" 2	Dark Cell 28 hours
Henry Barber	Ditto	" 2	Bread & Water 3 days
William Smith	Ditto	" 3	Ditto 2 days
Henry Perrett	Tearing Books	" 6	Dark Cell 24 hours
John Tilley	Talking	" 6	Bread & Water 1 Day
Peter De Lorm	Refusing to Work	" 7	Dark Cell 57 hours
John Dot	Insolence	" 8	Ditto 32 hours
John Brook	Idleness	" 11	Bread & Water 2 days
Robert Sheldon	Ditto	" 11	Ditto 3 days
William Cole	Ditto	" 11	Ditto
Thomas Lewis	Ditto	" 11	Ditto
Peter De Lorm	Refusing to Work	" 11	Dark Cell 3 days
Samuel Wheeler	Talking	" 13	Bread & Water 1 day

This page from a prison punishment book shows what happened to prisoners who did not behave themselves.
The most common 'crime' was

____

The most common punishment was

____

Some names appear more than once on this page alone.
Can you give at least two reasons why this might happen?

From wealth to poverty

3L

Spot the difference. These pictures are of the same Victorian family in the same room. They were quite well-off but then something happened. Look carefully at the pictures. *Can you work out what it was?*

List all of the things in the first picture that are also in the second. *Is there anything in the second picture that is not in the first?*

Tell the story of the two pictures. What happened? Why? The artist, George Cruikshank, drew more pictures to show what happened next. *Can you tell the end of the story?*

Victorian dress

4 TEACHERS NOTES

MASS production brought cheaper, ready-made clothes and greater fashion awareness. Women's pages began to appear in magazines and fashions became more widely publicised. Both the railway and the Royal Mail made mail-order possible and delivery speedy.

TECHNOLOGY and fashion often go hand in hand, so why not start with a simple scientific investigation? Collect different fabrics for sorting into natural and man-made. Which were unknown in Victorian times? If possible, compare the colour, pattern and feel of modern and nineteeth-century materials. Look at fashion changes and relate these changes to the changes in technology. (Fashion and technology can clash: girls working in the Potteries had a 'smashing' but expensive time when bustles were in vogue!) Follow the sequence hand-made/ machine-made/ factory-made.

A Victorian's clothes were a ready guide to status and wealth. Have the children investigate this by studying pictures. Is it true today?

Can you arrange demonstrations of smocking, lacemaking, beadwork or appliqué at school?

Dressing up

By borrowing or simply by being inventive, the children can dress themselves realistically in Victorian clothes. Caps, scarves and pinafores are not usually difficult to find but try to avoid obviously twentieth-century fabrics such as Nylon or Courtelle. Bowler hats, real lace, top hats, and Victorian spectacles are a bonus, so see what the children can bring from home. Work from photographs if you can; an old school photograph is ideal. Make sure that the children understand that a variety of dress existed, that fashions changed, that the differences between rich and poor were marked, and that there was a whole range of occupational dress. Sheets 4B/C, 5A/B, 6A/B will help. For a list of museums see page 7.

CLOTHES FOR MEN

A **smock** served as an overall and a general-purpose garment from the sixteenth to the present century. It was practical and comfortable attire for the working man.

How to make a smock

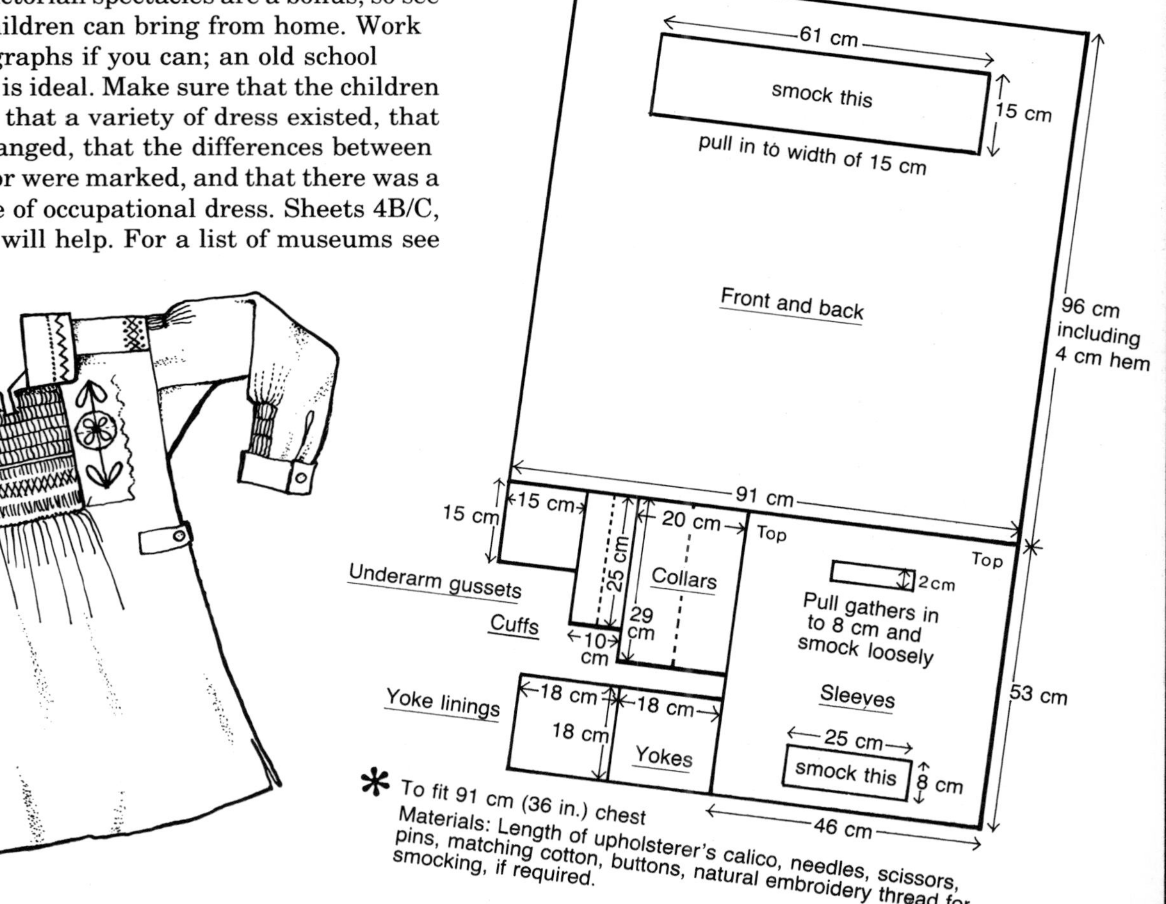

CLOTHES FOR MEN

Hats – straw hats, caps, or bowlers – were essential wear for most of the period. These can be improvised quite easily.

How to make a Panama hat

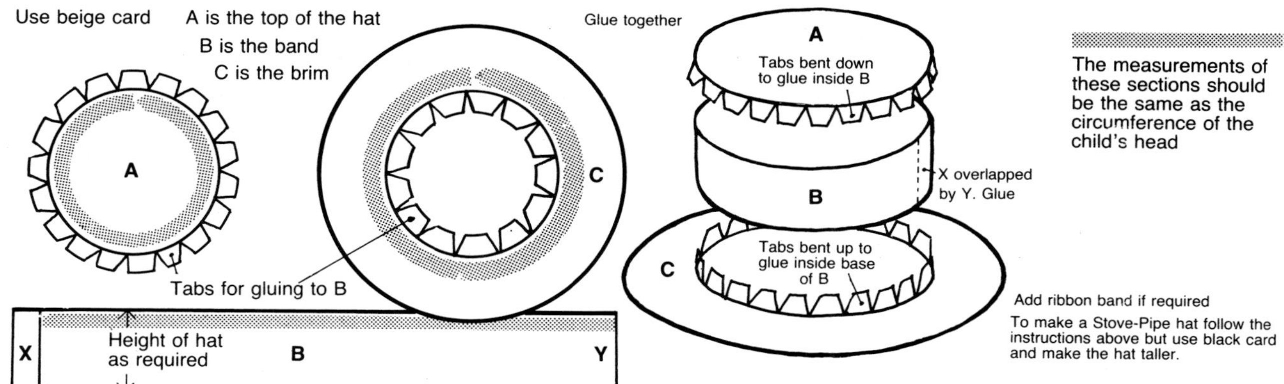

Sailor suits and **Eton collars** were very popular Sunday and holiday wear for boys towards the end of the century.

Scarves, neckerchiefs or mufflers kept sweat in and dust out during hard physical work. **Waistcoats** were worn by both men and boys. **Trousers** were worn sometimes with gaiters or with string tied below the knee, especially when working in the fields.

CLOTHES FOR WOMEN

Skirts were full length, of wool or cotton. An **apron** was worn to protect the skirt: white for best and sacking or dark green for heavy work. A **pinafore** was worn by young girls. It was set on a round or square yoke with frills, tucks and lace. A **shawl** was worn by poor women as an outer garment.

A **sunbonnet** belied its name as it tended to be worn all the year round, both indoors and out.

Mob caps were worn as a means of restraining the hair when working.

How to make a sunbonnet

How to make a Mob Cap

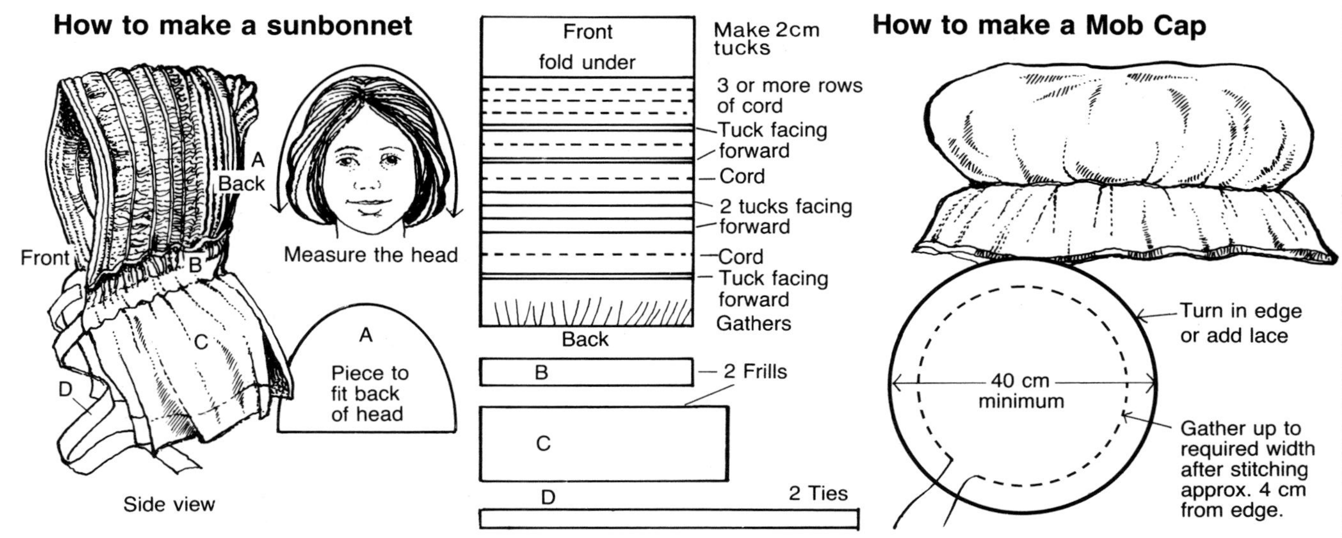

Victorian cut-out figures

Cut round these figures roughly at first.
Stick them on to card.
Now cut them out and stand them up.
Look at the smart clothes from about 1870 (sheet 4B) and the working clothes (sheet 4C).

Try to find out what colour they might have been. Colour them then cut them out. Dress the figures.
Collect photographs and drawings of Victorians. Use these to help you to make other sets of clothes in different styles.

FOLD UNDER

FOLD UNDER

Smart clothes

bouquet for
right hand

fold

fold

fold

fold

slit to go
over left
hand thumb

fold

fold

fold

fold

fold

fold

fold

slit for bouquet

fit cane
under hand

fold

fold

fold

fold

fold

fold

Working clothes

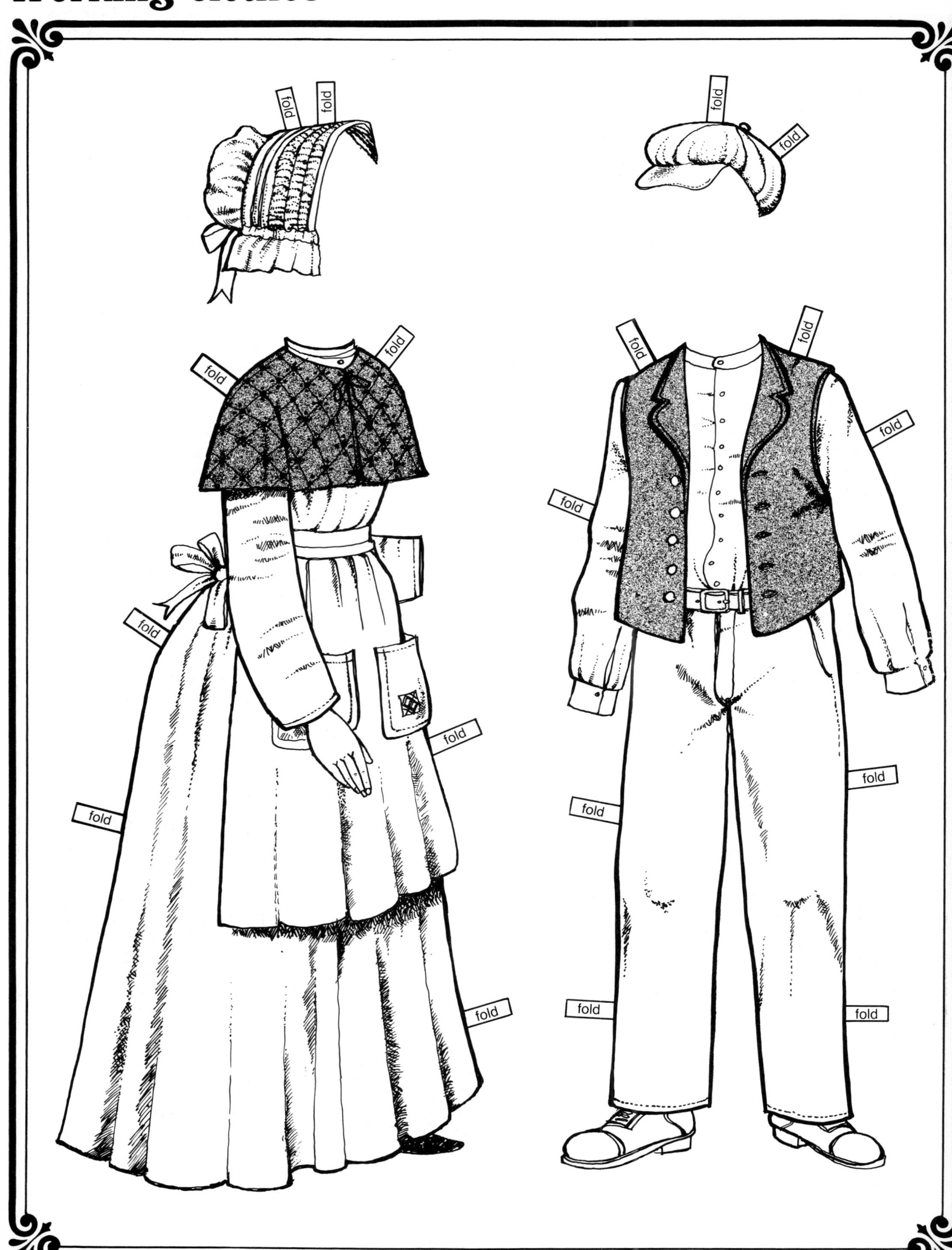

Victorian photographs

NO single person can be credited with the invention of photography, although the Frenchman J.N. Niepce (*nee-eps*) produced the first real photograph after an exposure of several hours (1826). Rapid progress was made in the development of the technology from 1840 onwards. One of the leading names in photography was William Henry Fox Talbot. He produced the first print from a negative (1838), allowing many prints to be made, and so originated a technique that is the basis of photography today. He produced the world's first photographically illustrated book, *Pencil of Nature* (1844). At Lacock, Wiltshire, where he lived, there is a museum of his work.

EARLY photographs required long exposure times. Coupled with the mechanical problems of camera operation, this meant that 40 seconds was an average sitting time. Children should try this for themselves (sheet 5A). Dressed in costume, they can attempt to simulate the straight-faced nineteenth-century portrait.

If you take photographs you will no doubt use a modern camera, but you can have sepia prints made for you (ask the processor who handles your film).

The children can make their own picture frames, decorated with shells (pasta shells will do) and sprayed silver.

You could explore the technology of photography further by making your own pinhole camera.

The problem of the galloping horse, as solved by Muybridge (*do* all of its feet leave the ground?), could be examined by the class. What other problems do they think that photography might help to solve?

Examine family albums for Victorian photographs. Look at the kind of records of your locality that were made by early photographers. Collectively the class could make a modern record of the local area. What sort of things would be of interest to children of the future?

The impact of photography was enormous. It began to affect politics through journalism. Every home had its family album. Science also benefited from the new technology.

Visits

The National Museum of Photography and Film in Bradford (British Museum and Bradford Council) must be one of the most wonderful museums in the country to take children to. Not every school will be able to visit, of course. Instead, perhaps you can find an enthusiastic photographer who will come into school to talk to the children. Using simple techniques, it is possible to develop and print black-and-white photographs in the classroom. (See Schools Council 5-13 *Holes, Gaps and Cavities Stages 1 and 2* and *Science, Models and Toys Stage 3*, Macdonald Education.)

How to make a Pinhole camera

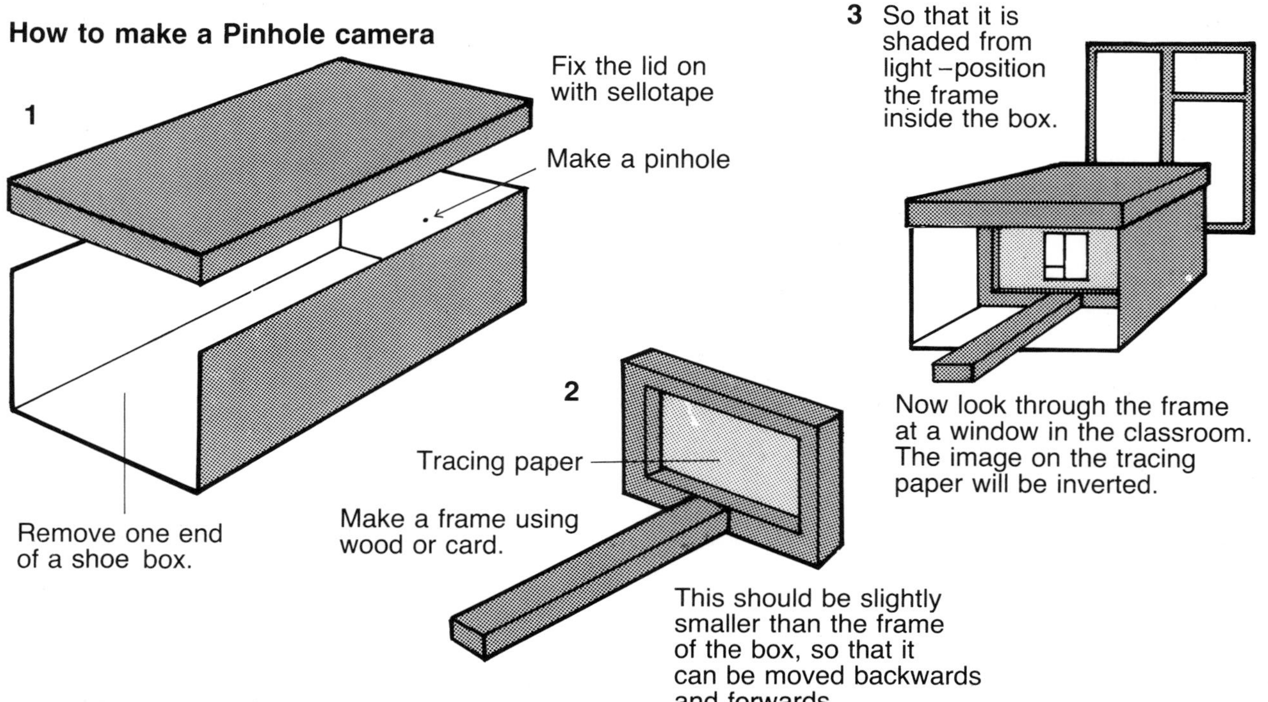
1
Fix the lid on with sellotape
Make a pinhole
Remove one end of a shoe box.
2
Tracing paper
Make a frame using wood or card.
This should be slightly smaller than the frame of the box, so that it can be moved backwards and forwards
3 So that it is shaded from light – position the frame inside the box.
Now look through the frame at a window in the classroom. The image on the tracing paper will be inverted.

Victorian photography: portraits

What differences are there between this portrait photograph and the sort that you normally have taken at school?
Can you explain the differences?

Taking a photograph then took more time than it does today. Work with a friend. Sit perfectly still for 40 seconds!
Can you smile for that long?

Sometimes a special hidden clamp around the neck was used to help to hold the person still. A mirror was also arranged so that sitters could see themselves. Try designing these things yourself. Remember that they must not be seen by the camera.

Clues from photographs

This was taken towards the end of the century when photography had improved and moving objects could be photographed.

In 1874, a girl wrote this letter to the *Englishwoman's Domestic Magazine*.

Compare your clothes with those of a child in the picture. Make two lists headed NOW and THEN.

> . . . I completed my fourteenth year last August. . . . I do not mind wearing short frocks, but I do think I am too old to wear strap shoes. I am a child, I know, but I am not a baby, and can keep my shoes on my feet without ankle straps. Do other girls of my age wear them? Mamma will only let me have white stockings.

What is she complaining about?
If you wrote a similar letter to a magazine today, what would you complain about?

THE Bryant & May match-girls strike (sheet 6A) was a major milestone along the road to equality for women. The author of the extract ('White Slavery', *Link*, 23 June 1888) on sheet 6A was a female journalist, Annie Besant. After publication, Bryant & May sacked the four girls held responsible for talking to the press. Immediately, 1400 match-girls came out on strike. The striking workers marched to Trafalgar Square. One song that they sang was:

All the publicity was bad. Questions were asked in Parliament. The employers were forced to capitulate and to take back the girls on more favourable terms. Amongst these was an undertaking to provide a separate place for eating, thus reducing the risk of 'phossy jaw' (necrosis of the jawbone with fatty degeneration of the kidney). After the strike the women formed a union, greatly encouraging women in other industries to do the same.

We'll hang out old Bryant on a sour apple tree,
We'll hang out old Bryant on a sour apple tree,
We'll hang out old Bryant on a sour apple tree,
As we go marching in . . .

(Tune: *John Brown's Body*)

Status of women in the nineteenth century

THE working woman was generally regarded as cheap and biddable labour. All classes of women were disadvantaged when compared with men. They had no vote, few property rights and rarely achieved financial independence. Access to public life was very limited indeed. The position of the Queen-Empress was a strange irony. However, there was support for as well as opposition to an improvement in women's status. In 1866, John Stuart Mill proposed that women be given the vote. Schools and University Colleges for women were founded in the 1840s and 1850s. Married Women's Property Acts (1870 and 1882) allowed women to keep property which previously had become their husbands' on marriage. Demographic trends mid-century were such that only about one woman in four was likely to marry. Many sought satisfaction in a career. Opportunities opened up in local government and women were particularly active in social reform. Nevertheless, at the end of the century, they still lacked the vote, and were officially excluded from many professions. Over one-tenth of employed females were in domestic service.

- The story of the match-girls cries out for dramatisation. You might try letting the children script scenes, using the sequence of events provided by their own 'comic strip' (sheet 6A).
- Debate the rights and wrongs of the case. Are there any modern parallels? Discuss the role of women in society today.
- Write newspaper articles exposing an injustice, or collect articles about them.
- Dress up a child as a match-girl and use her as a subject for sketching or painting.
- Compile a biographical dictionary of nineteenth-century women. Each child, or group of children, researches one entry, producing text and illustrations. The book should be bound and covered, and have proper title pages, introduction, and so on. The names below provide a start.

FAMOUS WOMEN

Dorothea Beale	*Educational reformer*
Isabella Beeton	*Author*
Annie Besant	*Writer, and campaigner in India*
Isabel Bird Bishop	*Explorer*
Brontë sisters	*Novelists*
Elizabeth Barrett Browning	*Poet*
Frances Buss	*Educational reformer*
Mary Carpenter	*Social reformer*
Grace Darling	*Shipwreck heroine*
George Eliot (Mary Ann Evans)	*Novelist*
Millicent Fawcett	*Campaigner for voting rights*
Elizabeth Fry	*Prison reformer*
Elizabeth Gaskell	*Novelist*
Kate Greenaway	*Book illustrator*
Octavia Hill	*Housing reformer and founder of the National Trust*
Sophia Jex-Blake	*Pioneer of medical education for wome*
Mary Kingsley	*Traveller, writer and nurse*
Jenny Lind	*Singer and professor of music*
Harriet Martineau	*Novelist and journalist*
Hannah More	*Poet, writer and humanitarian*
Florence Nightingale	*Nursing pioneer*
Ellen Terry	*Actress*
Beatrice Webb	*Social reformer, economist*

- The children can make models of women at work using sheet 6B.

The match-girls' strike

In the summer of 1888, four women workers at the Bryant & May match factory in London talked to newspaper reporters. They told of terrible conditions at the factory. This is part of what was published.

The hour for commencing work is 6.30 in summer and 8 in winter; work concludes at 6 p.m. Half an hour is allowed for breakfast and an hour for dinner. The young girl workers have to stand the whole time.

Typical is a 16-year old *piece worker* who earns 4 s. [20p] a week. She pays 2 s. for the rent of the one room where she lives. The child lives on only bread-and-butter and tea, alike for breakfast and dinner.

The splendid salary of 4 s. is subject to fines if the feet are dirty, or the ground under the bench is left untidy. Some departments fine 3 d. [over 1p] for talking. One girl was fined 1 s. for letting the web twist round a machine in an attempt to save her fingers from being cut, and was sharply told, 'Take care of the machine, never mind your fingers.' The foreman clouts them when he is mad.

The girls eat their food in the rooms in which they work, so that the fumes of the *phosphorus* mix with their poor meal and they eat disease. The phosphorus poison works on them as they chew and rots away the [jaw] bone. The foremen have sharp eyes. If they see a girl's face, swell, they know the sign and she is sent off and gets no pay during her absence.

Can you guess what the employers did after this appeared in the newspapers?
Write your own ending to the story.
Can you find out what really happened?

Draw small pictures, just like a comic strip, to tell the story of 'a day in the life of a match-girl'. Add captions if you wish. Act out the story with a group of friends.

Piece worker: one who is paid for work by the piece or quantity, not by time
Phosphorus: a yellow, poisonous, easily burned substance used in making matches

Women at work

6B

Magazine seller | Cook | Coal-miner | Nanny

Which is which? Can you match the names correctly?

These Victorian women will make good clay models.

You will need:

A small bottle (a fizzy drink bottle will do)
Vaseline
Damp newspaper
Clay
Heavy rolling pin
Clay tools
Paint and varnish or glaze for decoration

Cover the bottle first with Vaseline, then closely and smoothly with a layer of damp newspaper.

Roll out the clay to about ½ cm thick and cut into rectangles. These should now be wrapped around the bottle to form the basic shape of the figure.

Add 'sausage' arms, a head, and other parts as you go along.

Rough-up and dampen any parts to be joined and fix them firmly, otherwise the model will fall apart when it dries.

Shape the figure firmly with your fingers and use the clay tools for fine details.

When the model is completely dry, the bottle can be carefully removed. Paint and varnish the model or fire it in a kiln and glaze it.

Servants

Wealthy Victorians had servants.
How many servants does Mrs Beeton mention in this passage from her 'Book of Household Management'?

The first duty of the housemaid in winter is to open the shutters of all the lower rooms in the house, and take up the hearthrugs in those rooms which she is going to *'do'* before breakfast. . . . After the shutters are all opened, she sweeps the breakfast-room, sweeping the dust towards the fireplace, of course previously removing the *fender*. She should then lay a cloth (generally made of coarse *wrappering*) over the carpet in front of the stove, and on this should place her housemaid's box, containing black-lead brushes, leathers, emery-paper, cloth, black-lead, and all utensils necessary for cleaning a grate, with the cinder-pail on the other side. She now sweeps up the ashes, and deposits them in her cinder-pail, ... The cinders disposed of, she proceeds to black-lead the grate. Having blackened, brushed and polished every part, and made all clean and bright, she now proceeds to lay the fire. . . .

The several fires lighted, the housemaid proceeds with her dusting, and polishing the several pieces of furniture in the breakfast parlour, leaving no corner unvisited. Before sweeping the carpet, it is a good practice to sprinkle it all over with tea-leaves, which not only lay all dust, but give a slightly fragrant smell to the room. It is now in order for the reception of the family, and where there is neither footman nor parlour-maid, she now proceeds to the dressing-room, and lights her mistress's fire, if she is in the habit of having one to dress by. Her mistress is called, hot water placed in the dressing-room for her use, her clothes – as far as they are under the housemaid's charge – put before the fire, hanging a fire-guard on the bars where there is one, while she proceeds to prepare the breakfast.

Newspaper advertisements for housemaids as well as giving details of wages and hours, usually demanded 'good character' and 'no followers'.
What did this mean?

Write an advertisement for a housemaid.

Do: clean
Fender: a guard before a hearth to keep in the ashes
Wrappering: material

A Victorian corner in the classroom 7

TEACHERS NOTES

Create a Victorian interior

GAIN insights into Victorian life and provide a 'set' for drama or 'pretending'. It is a way of using many of the objects that children bring into the classroom and can be an alternative to a class museum. You can begin with an object, perhaps obtained from a local museum, and build up an interior around it. You can join in the process of discovery with the children. Involve them in making the decisions. Which type of home are you going to recreate? Which room? Collect together as many illustrations as you can, so that you and the class know what you are aiming to produce.

Items such as pots, pans and copper kettles, wash tubs and dollys, may be borrowed or made. A trolley can easily be transformed into a kitchen range (sheet 7B) and a grandfather clock made from boxes. Wallpaper can be printed by making a block from a thin polystyrene tile. Cut out the design (it can be pressed out with a sharp pencil) and stick the tile on to a piece of wood to make a firm printing block.

With corrugated card, a few sticks, black paper and red/orange tissue, you have the makings of a fine fireplace. Do not forget the photographs or silhouettes, clocks, mirrors and candlesticks.

Objects such as old irons, kettles and pans will quickly give a 'kitchen feel' to a room. A washing line with mob cap, long knickers, etc. will add extra authenticity.

If you do recreate a kitchen, have the servants' uniforms (aprons, caps, etc.) on hand so that the children can dress up for role play. A list of jobs could be left out for servants to 'do': beating a carpet (outside), polishing brass, dusting with a feather duster, carrying buckets of water with a yoke, and using a brush and shovel (scatter damp tea-leaves on the floor to collect the dust).

This type of work can easily take over the classroom, so choose your site carefully – a corridor perhaps? Invite parents and take them on a Victorian tour: 'Open Day at Bleak House' or 'What the Butler Really Saw'. Make it a living exhibition of what the children have learned. Act out small scenes; they need not all be scripted. Let the butler show in the visitors (everyone should try to be in costume).

Where projects are shared by classes, there is the chance of creating several different rooms. You could pretend to be showing prospective buyers around a house. Produce estate agents' guides, have the housemaid at work, the family singing in the parlour, etc.

Sheets 7A, 7B and 12A will be useful when creating a Victorian setting but they can also stand as valid activities on their own.

(A dado, as mentioned in sheet 7A, is a skirting of wood along the lower part of the walls of a room, often merely represented by wallpaper, painting, etc.)

Stencils

7A

Victorians often used patterns to decorate their homes. These patterns were made by using **stencils** – pieces of card or metal with a design cut out of them.

When paint was put on the stencil, the paint went through the holes and made the pattern. The stencil could be used again and again to make a border along a wall or round a piece of furniture.

Some patterns were plain and simple but some were like these.

Stencilled patterns were often painted above the dado (*day-doh*) in a Victorian room.
Can you find out where the dado is?
Do you know any rooms that still have a dado?

Sometimes the patterns were used to make a 'pretend' dado.
Can you think why?

Photocopy, or transfer, this design on to card or tough paper.
Use stencil brushes if you have them.

You can use the pattern for decorating boxes, folders or other things in class, or when making a Victorian room.

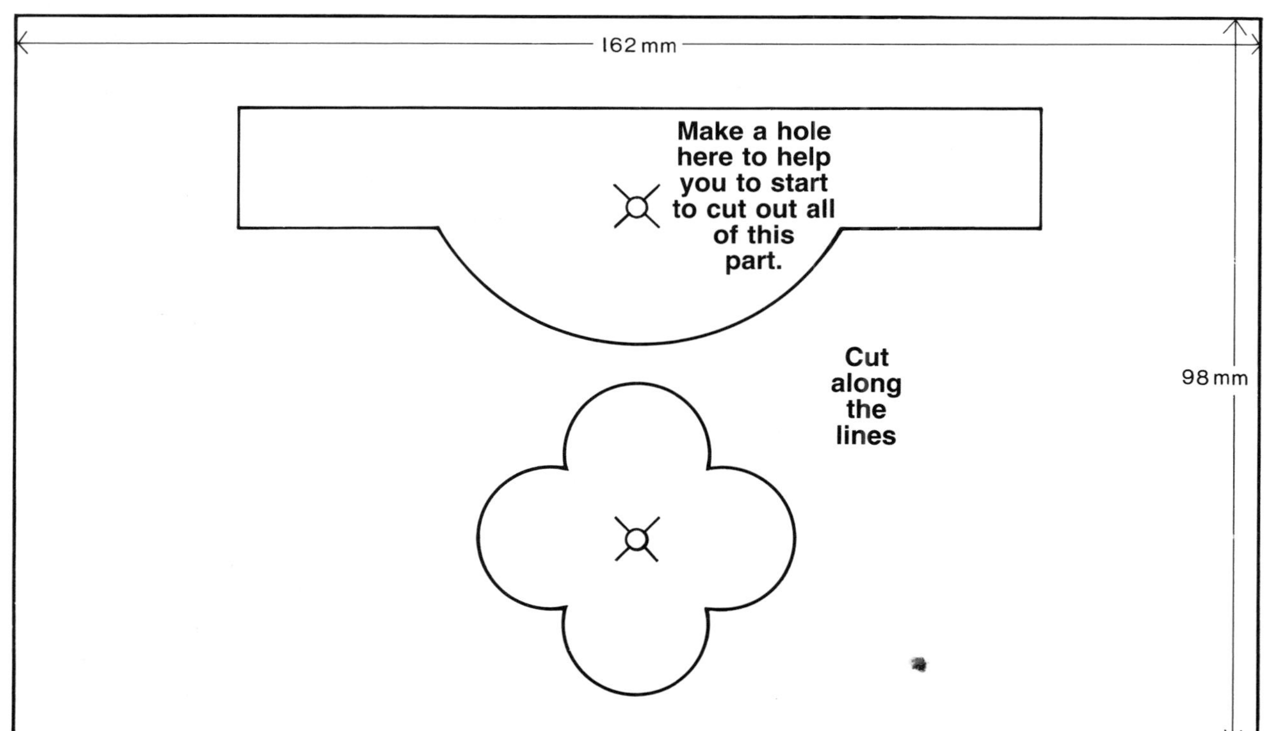
162 mm
98 mm
Make a hole here to help you to start to cut out all of this part.
Cut along the lines

A kitchen range

Cast-iron kitchen ranges were used in large nineteenth-century houses. *Can you see how the range worked?* Match the descriptions **a–g** to the correct parts numbered **1–7.**

a Hot water came from the tap on the boiler which was heated by being next to the fire.

b Ash was emptied from this tray.

c Smoke went up this chimney.

d This handle could be used to close the opening in the chimney, and so force hot air to go around the oven instead of up the chimney.

e Main fire and grate.

f Oven door.

g Iron rings could be lifted off for cleaning and to let kettles boil more quickly.

Can you see any problems in using this range?

LARGE numbers of people left the British Isles for Canada, South Africa, New Zealand, Australia (all in the Empire) and, of course, America. Australia was used as a dumping ground for convicts but, as early as 1839, there were more free settlers there than convicts. A steady outflow of transported persons continued, the most famous being the Tolpuddle Martyrs.

Dorset farm labourers, led by George Loveless, tried to form a Union branch when wages were lowered from 8 s. (40p) to 7 s. (35p) a week. At Dorchester, in 1834, they were found guilty, not of forming a Union, but of taking an illegal oath. Six men, including Loveless, were transported to Tasmania for seven years. They were pardoned in 1836.

The five Tolpuddle Martyrs pictured were those that returned from Australia to Britain in 1838. The missing martyr is James Hammett, about whom least is known. He was the last man home, delayed possibly by a secondary charge of assault in Australia. He arrived back by free passage in August 1839, the others having returned to England in March 1838.

Boosts were given to emigration figures by disasters such as the Irish Famine (1845-49) when the potato crop failed. About a million people died and a further two million emigrated (see population figures for Prescot, sheet 3D). The development of steamships considerably speeded up the journey to America. Between 1870 and 1900, some 21 million people left Europe to start new lives abroad, about half of these going to America. Opportunities in the 'new' countries abounded, particularly in agriculture, and sometimes offers of free land were made to settlers.

Transportation

THE story of the Tolpuddle Martyrs provides a vivid illustration of how harshly those who were transported were treated. The story could be told in pictures or as a dramatic 'radio' broadcast of the trial and of the voyage to Tasmania. Further to sheet 8B, children could make up a prisoner's description of the type recorded for the Tolpuddle Martyrs. Use this as an example.

No. 1576/62 Brine James; *Aged* 21; *Education* – R.W. [Reads and Writes]; *Religion* – Protestant; Unmarried; *Native Place* – Dorsetshire; *Trade* – Farm servant; *Offence* – unlawful oaths; *Tried* – Dorset Assizes, 14 March, 1833; *Sentence* – 7 years; *Previous convictions* – none; *Height* – 5 ft 5 in; *Complexion* – ruddy; *Hair* – brown; *Eyes* – hazel-grey; *Physical details* – scar right eyebrow. Scar under left nostril. Scar on back of left thumb, scars on face and one on back of middle finger left hand.

Emigration

Emigration might be dealt with by means of imaginative work, through painting, drama and poetry. What is it like to leave one's native land for good? Discuss the notion of the 'New World' (listen to Dvorak's symphony). What would you most like to take with you to a foreign land? What would you remember most vividly of home?

The extract below is from an interview with an official of the British Women's Emigration Association.

'The Association has been in existence about ten years', Mrs. Vincent informed our representative. 'The object is to provide openings for working women of good character in Canada, South Africa, and West Australia. We secure for our emigrants proper protection on the voyage, and arrange for them to be met on their arrival. It is also our aim to keep the girls in sight for a year or two after their emigration, so that they may not feel themselves altogether forsaken and forgotten by their friends at home. During 1893 the Association sent out 176 single women, besides eleven families.'

'What colony received the largest number?'

'Canada stands first, with 68; then West Australia, with 42; and next South Africa, with 30. To the United States we sent 20, and to New Zealand 19. Matrons are sent out in charge of the different parties, and their fares are paid for by the Society for Promoting Christian Knowledge, except in the case of those on the West Australian ships, who are provided for by the Government of the colony. The presence of the matrons gives a guarantee that no harm will befall the young travellers on the voyage.

'A companion help from South Africa says:

> "I live a very out-of-door life, getting up early and going for a long ride with my pupil, aged twelve; and again, after school is over, we walk and play tennis, if not too hot. You ought to impress on all the girls that think of coming out here that they will have to turn their hands to anything and everything. I had to cook, sweep, dust, any amount of needlework, scrub, act as nurse to two young children. The places that seem to be most vacant are those for nurses, and ladies are generally preferred. One has many unpleasant things to put up with, especially at first, but if you are good-tempered and obliging, and do your duty, any girl can get on. I have been out here ten months now, and must say I am very happy and comfortable."

'Great care has to be exercised in selecting suitable emigrants,' Mrs. Vincent continued; 'and unless the character is strong and self-reliant, I should hesitate before advising a young woman to leave her home. But for a girl who loves the open air and has a spice of adventure in her nature, the free life of these young colonies offers many advantages. For myself, if I had to choose between slavery for a paltry pittance in some "shabby genteel" situation at home, and seeking my fortune in the far North-West, or in some thriving Australasian city, I should thankfully accept the opportunity which the Emigration Society offers. Those who wish further information about the openings for working women in the colonies should apply by letter or in person to Miss Lefroy, 11 Imperial Institute, South Kensington, London.'

Teachers should read this extract and discuss it with the class. Unfamiliar words will need explanation. Why did women need an organisation to protect their interests? Which sort of woman was being encouraged to emigrate? Who was most likely to read this article?

After discussion and background work, children should write letters home from abroad in the role of a female emigrant. What was the journey like? What difficulties did they face?

Emigrants from Britain

Vast numbers of people left Britain permanently in the nineteenth century.
Can you find out where they emigrated to?
Mark on the map the main countries where they settled.

Find out as much as you can about how they travelled.
List the reasons why someone might wish to emigrate.

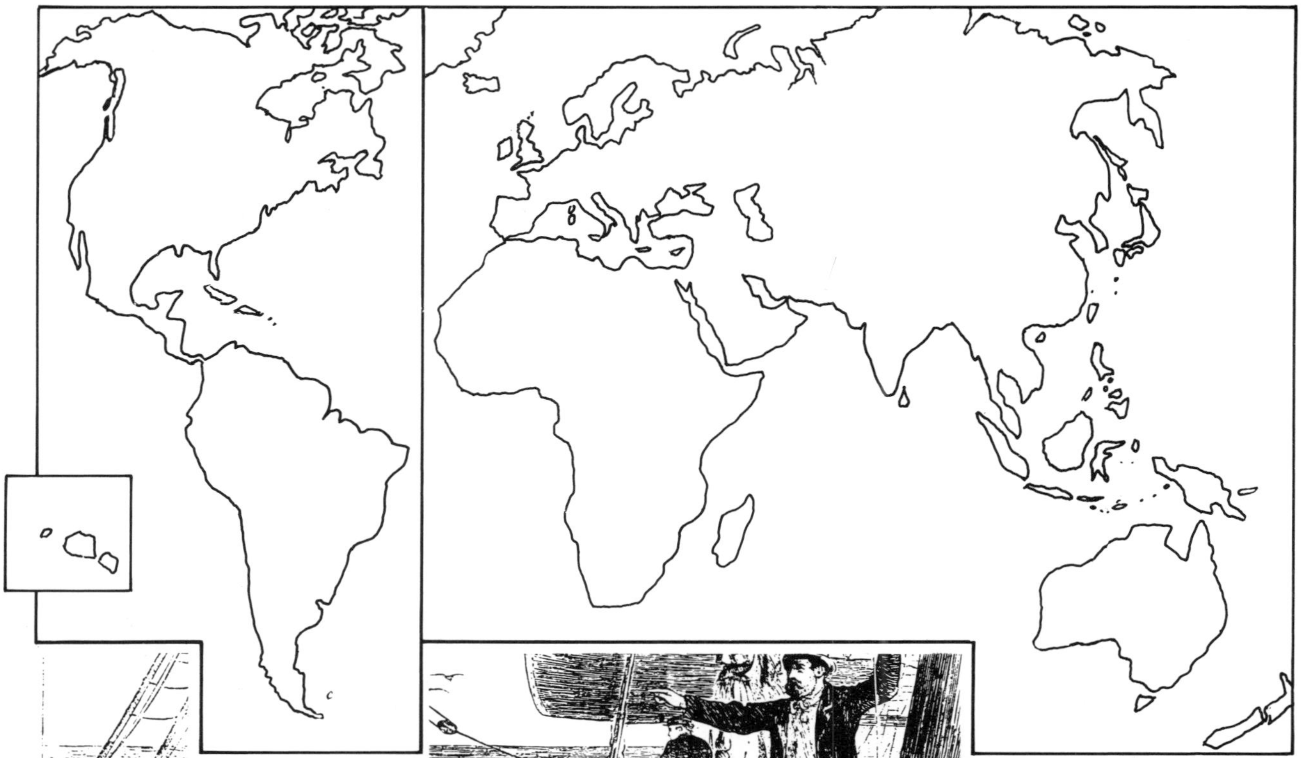

Transportation

Try to read this handwritten letter. (If you get stuck, look at the printed words.)

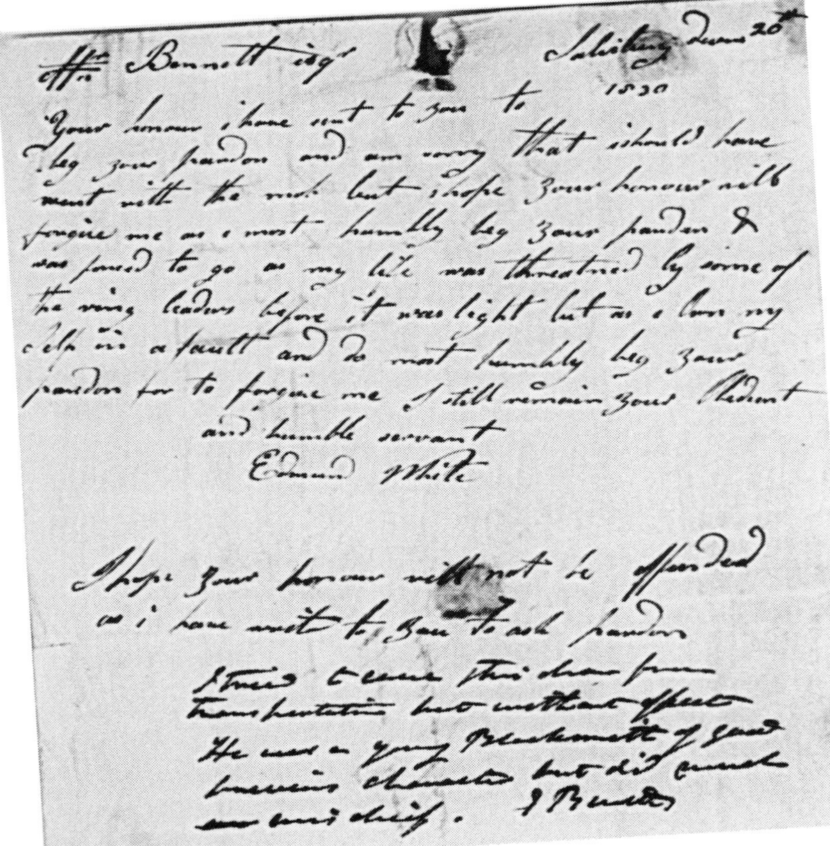

Mr. Bennett esqr

Salisbury december 20th 1830

Your honour i have sent to you to
beg your pardon and am sorry that i should have
went with the mob but i hope your honour will
forgive me as i most humbly beg your pardon &
was forced to go as my life was threatened by some of
the ring leaders before it was light but as i Own my
Self in a fault and do most humbly beg your
pardon for to forgive me I still remain your Obedient
and humble servant

Edmund White

I hope your honour will not be offended
as i have writ to you to ask pardon.

*I tried to save this Man from
transportation but without effect.
He was a young Blacksmith of good
previous character but did much
mischief.* *J. Bennett*

The letter was dated ____________

Edmund White worked as a ____________

He wrote to ____________

because ____________

____

In the end his punishment was

____

What had Edmund White done?
Design a wanted notice for Edmund White describing his crime.

Up to the middle of the nineteenth century, people could be sentenced to transportation for quite small crimes.
Do you think that someone who poached a rabbit to feed a starving family should have been punished in this way?

Childhood and education

THE contrast between rich and poor was particularly marked in the Victorian era, so childhood experiences varied widely. The idea of treating childhood as something special and different began to evolve. More books for children began to appear, as well as manufactured toys, some with Empire connections (e.g. toy soldiers).

Most people felt it right or necessary to send children out to work as soon as possible (see sheet 3G). However, middle-class consciences, and a need for a more educated workforce, sustained the pressure which led to the Factory and Education Acts. Religion, death and discipline were more familiar features of childhood than they are today. School log books record not only high levels of religion in the curriculum and the involvement of the local clergy but also frequent physical punishment. Infant mortality, for all classes, was very high (see sheets 3E and 3F).

Timeline

1837 Accession of Queen Victoria

1846 Pupil-teacher system introduced: a form of training for teachers, with grants and 7.5 hours of training per week.

1856 Publication of *Tom Brown's Schooldays* (Thomas Hughes)

1862 Revised Code: education grants to schools, subject to satisfactory pupils' attendance figures and to the testing of the '3 R's' by an Inspector (payment by results). This saved money and increased school attendance but it encouraged mechanical methods of learning, lowered the status and morale of teachers, narrowed the curriculum, and over-pressurised pupil and teacher alike. The Code was finally abolished in 1897.

1865 Publication of *Alice's Adventures in Wonderland* (Charles Dodgson alias Lewis Carroll)

1870 Forster's Elementary Education Act: School Boards established schools where required, mostly in urban areas. The Boards were empowered to charge weekly fees. The Act was intended to fill gaps in a system that relied on the Churches but it also stimulated voluntary efforts to establish schools. This dual system of state and voluntary schools still exists.

1874 Factory Act: raised to 10 years the age at which a child could be employed in a factory. It implied compulsory schooling for those below 10 years but there were many loopholes. School Boards passed by-laws making attendance compulsory, so that, by 1876, 84 per cent of children in towns were under compulsion, although in rural areas the figure was 50 per cent.

Finding the evidence

School log books (sheets 9E and 9F) or photocopies can be obtained from the County Archivist. If your school log book is held by the archivist, try to borrow the originals. **Punishment books** are interesting if you can find them. **Hymn books** are full of Victorian hymns, which might be a good starting-point for an RE project.

Admission registers are very useful but you need a fair number of entries to do any kind of analysis. Early registers include details of father's occupation as well as addresses. Analyse entries by name or occupation (tallying, reading, graphing). Computer programs that handle and sort data are excellent for this, and you can simultaneously tackle a National Curriculum mathematics attainment target (See p.22).

This can lead to research into Parish Registers, gravestones, etc. Information can be gleaned on health, jobs, weather, and absenteeism. You may be able to trace the history of a family that is still represented in the school. Try to re-people the school for a particular date in the last century so that, if you have a Victorian day, everybody can be a real person.

Comparing then with now

Examine a Victorian school. Compare documentary evidence with evidence on the ground. Compare a modern school with an old one. Look at heating, lighting and the physical arrangement of the school and at timetabling, curriculum, class sizes, lunch arrangements, and so on. Perhaps you can build up a timeline of important dates in the history of your school.

Setting up a class Museum of Childhood is a good way of coping with the artefacts that the children will bring in. Organise it like a proper museum with a catalogue and information cards. Christening robes (ask the local vicar to explain about and perhaps demonstrate christening), lemonade bottles, old story books, etc. will make an impressive display. You could trace the development of particular exhibits up to the present day (see notes on timelines, page 8).

History and drama

'Drama' tends to see the past only in terms of conflict or exciting happenings, when in fact there was a great deal of monotony, but why not simply pretend? Organise a pretend schoolday. The adventurous might like to pretend in costume. Consult some old school photographs and improvise (see pages 36–7 and sheets 4A and 4B). Make the children line up in the playground, inspect hands and shoes, and make the sexes enter by different entrances. You can convert your classroom into the required setting with mock wood-panelling for the walls, high-placed imitation windows, oil lamps and stove. Globes, abaci, religious paintings and a picture of Queen Victoria can be added. (For more suggestions for a Victorian setting, see page 49.)

Log books sometimes contain detailed syllabuses, which are very helpful (sheet 9F). Learn playground games, memorise poetry, try cursive writing (sheet 9C), chant spellings. Do old-fashioned arithmetic, drill (P.E.), or an 'object' lesson (One log book reads: 'This week's object lesson was the elephant'). Use slates if you can. These can be bought from toy and gift shops. Sand trays can be improvised, using the lid of a shoe box.

('Parsing', as mentioned in the extract on sheet 9F means breaking down sentences into their component grammatical parts.)

If you do require a dramatic focus for the day, arrange for the School Inspector to visit unexpectedly (no doubt you can find someone suitably imposing to carry off the role!) or you might prefer to have the vicar's daughter inspect the sewing. Do not forget to finish off the day with prayers and the distribution of merit certificates.

Another approach which works well is the re-enactment of a specific event: Queen Victoria's Jubilee (see page 10) or the opening of the school or a park. Children can help with the research. Parents will usually join in and will even turn up in costume!

Art and craft

A large collage of a school playground with Victorian games being played will involve the children in further historical research. Place the smaller figures near the back and wrought-iron railings, cut out of black paper, along the front. A stencilled border is effective (see sheet 7A). Breughel's sixteenth-century painting, 'Children's Games', is worth examining; little had changed!

Romantic but useful scenes of Victorian childhood are depicted on a number of modern birthday cards (for example, see ranges by Medici). See also sheets 11A and 10B.

Make coloured blotting paper into booklets. Decorate the front and use them as gifts. (What does it mean 'to blot your copy book'?)

Design a decorative tract for the classroom wall: 'Be good sweet maid and let who can be clever' or similar.

Make a zig-zag ABC book. Each child chooses a letter of the alphabet and makes up a rhyming couplet about it and illustrates it. Extra children can do the cover or put the book together.

Books

Growing up in Victorian Days, M. Harrison, Wayland 1980

Toys in History, A. Schofield, Wayland 1978 (OP*)

Victorian Kinetic Toys and How to Make Them, P. and C. F. Sayer, Evans 1977 (OP*)

Growing up in Victorian Britain, S. Ferguson, Batsford 1977

Children at Work, Then and There series, E. Longmate, Longman 1981

At School in 1900, S. Purkis, Into the Past series, Longman 1981

The Illustrated Victorian Songbook, R. Hunter (ed.), Michael Joseph 1984

Finding out about Victorian Schools, A. Clarke, Batsford 1983

Harrods Store Catalogue 1895, reprinted by David & Charles

*OP = out of print

Filmstrip

Victorian Children, BBC Radio, 1 Portland Place, London W1A 1AA

Visits

Armley Mill Industrial Museum, Leeds. (0532) 637861
Factory classroom; full-time teacher attached for Leeds schools

Edinburgh Museum of Childhood. (031) 225 2424
Good exhibits

Museum of Childhood,
Cambridge Heath Road, Bethnal Green, London E2 9PA. (01) 980 2415
Excellent range of exhibits

St Fagan's Welsh Folk Museum, Cardiff. (0222) 397951
Complete old school with furniture, playground games, etc.

Sudbury Hall Museum of Childhood,
Sudbury, Derbyshire. (028378) 305
School within the country house, established before state education. Victorian lessons in dress can be arranged. Contact the Education Officer at the house. Parties need to be booked one term in advance.

Schoolwork: reading and games

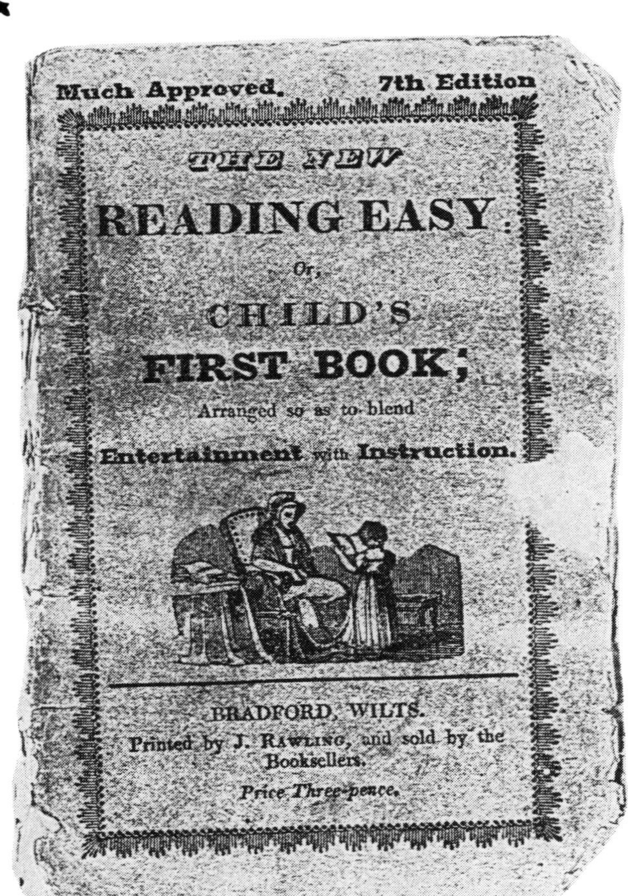

Much Approved. 7th Edition

THE NEW

READING EASY:

Or,

CHILD'S

FIRST BOOK;

Arranged so as to blend

Entertainment with Instruction.

BRADFORD, WILTS.

Printed by J. Rawling, and sold by the Booksellers.

Price Three-pence.

ADVERTISEMENT.

IN the following arrangement, the Publisher has had in view progression. How far he has succeeded in directing the young mind from the joining of two letters to easy lessons, and from thence to entertaining tales, he must leave the Governess or Tutor to determine. He begs leave, however, to state, that it has been his study to make every page in this little book of importance to the Child, not inserting any thing merely for the purpose of filling up, so much the fault of many works of this kind, to the manifest drawback of the child, and grief of the teacher.

Fanny Beale
the gift of her
Grandmother
1848

This is the front cover and introduction of a typical Victorian school book.
Who did it belong to?

Examine the cover.
What two things does the book aim to do?

Read this from the book.
Do you think that it ***instructs*** *and* ***entertains*** *as it says on the cover?*

Do you agree with what the book says about the games?
Describe them in your own words. Change anything that you do not agree with.

Or, Child's First Book. 25

FLYING a KITE.

In fine weather it is pleasant for a good boy to walk in the fields, to fly his kite, but he must be careful to hold it firm lest it should fly away from him.

BALLS.

To toss up and down a hand ball is amusing, but to play at foot ball is dangerous. I advise every good boy to avoid such a rough game, if he wishes to have his legs and feet kept from injury.

BLIND-MAN'S-BUFF.

This also is a very dangerous exercise, because the boy or girl that is blinded, may run into great danger, or otherwise do a deal of mischief.

DOLLS.

This is play for a little girl. To have some pretty clothes to dress her doll with, and a little bed to lie it in, is very amusing. I have heard of a little girl who tried to make her doll spell and read; although she could not accomplish her wishes with the pains she took, she forwarded her own learning.

Schoolwork: moral tales

The Victorians loved moral tales (stories that taught about right and wrong). This story is from a school textbook.

True Duncan

1. There was once a little boy named Duncan. The boys used to call him 'True Duncan', because he would never tell a lie. One day he was playing with an axe in the school-yard. The axe was used for cutting the wood for the school-room fire in winter.

2. While Duncan was chopping a stick, the teacher's cat, Old Tabby, came and leaped on to the log of wood where Duncan was at work. He had raised the axe to cut the wood, but it fell on the cat and killed her. What to do he knew not. She was the master's pet, and used to sit on a cushion at his side while he was hearing the boys their lessons.

3. Duncan stood looking at poor Tabby. His face grew red, and the tears stood in his eyes. All the boys came running up, and every one had something to say. One of them was heard whispering to the others, 'Now, boys, let us see if Duncan can't make up a fib as well as the rest of us.' – 'Not he,' said Tom Brown, who was Duncan's friend, 'not he; I'll warrant Duncan will be true as gold.'

4. John Jones stepped up and said, 'Come, boys; let us fling the cat into the lane, and we can tell Mr Cole that the butcher's dog killed her. You know that he worried her last week.' Some of them thought that that would do very well. But Duncan looked quite angry. His cheeks swelled, and his face grew redder than before. 'No! no!' said he. 'Do you think I would say that? It would be a *lie* – a LIE!' Each time he used the word his voice grew louder.

5. Then he took up the poor thing and carried her into the school-room. The boys followed, to see what would happen. The master looked up and said, 'What is this? my poor Tabby killed? Who could have done me such an injury?'

6. All were silent for a little while. As soon as Duncan could get his voice, he said, 'Mr Cole, I am very sorry. I killed poor Tabby. Indeed, sir, I am *very* sorry. I ought to have been more careful, for I saw her rubbing herself against the log. I am more sorry than I can tell, sir.'

7. Every one expected to see Mr Cole get very angry, take down his cane, and give Duncan a sound thrashing. But instead of that, he put on a pleasant smile and said, 'Duncan, you are a brave boy! I saw and heard all that passed in the yard, from my window above. I am glad to see such an example of truth and honour in my school.'

8. Duncan took out his handkerchief and wiped his eyes. The boys couldn't keep silence any longer; and when Tom Brown cried, 'Three cheers for True Duncan,' they all joined, and made the school-house ring with a hearty hurrah.

9. The teacher then said, 'My boys, I am glad you know what is right, and that you approve it; though I am afraid some of you could not have done it. Learn from this time that nothing can make a lie necessary. Suppose Duncan had taken your evil advice, and come to me with a lie: it would have been instantly detected, and instead of the honour of truth, he would have had only the shame of falsehood.'

1. Why was a boy called 'True Duncan'? 2. What happened when Duncan was chopping a stick? 3. What did one of the boys say? What was Tom Brown's reply? 4. What did John Jones propose? What did Duncan say? 5. What did he do? 6. What did he say? 7. What did Mr Cole say? 8. How did the boys receive the teacher's words? 9. What did the teacher then say?

After reading this, the children had to write their own story about telling the truth. *Can you write a similar moral tale?*

Schoolwork: copybook and rules

Teachers used every opportunity, even handwriting lessons, to encourage children to be good. Try these copy exercises for yourself. Write on the lines below.
Can you explain what each saying means?

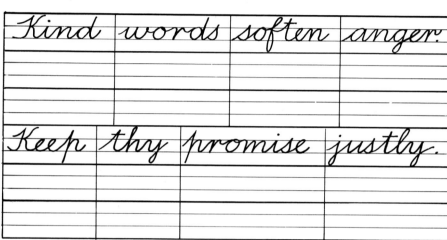

Kind	words	soften	anger.

Keep	thy	promise	justly.

RULES FOR PUPILS

I.

Prepare your lessons carefully.

II.

Come *regularly* and *punctually* to School.

III.

Be as *tidy* as possible in your dress.

IV.

If you do not understand what is taught, ask your Teacher to explain it.

V.

Be *respectful* and *attentive* to your Teachers, and remember how kind it is of them to take so much trouble with you.

VI.

Speak the *truth* at all costs.

VII.

Be respectful and obedient to your Parents, Guardians, Teachers, and all set over you.

VIII.

Study to be polite and courteous to all, avoiding coarseness and rudeness.

IX.

Fight against *selfishness, anger,* and *all* evil.

X.

Be kind and obliging to every one.

Do you think these are good rules?
Would you add any others?

Off school

		Brought forward	1453
Moore Arthur	II	Rheumatic fever	27
Dobson William	V	Congestion of lungs & pleurisy	10
Heath Frederic	III	Ring-worm	28
Carpenter Henry	III	Debility with chest cough	18
Platts William	II	"Mumps"	22
Monk George	V	Broken arm	11
Pearce Frederic	II	Inflammation of lungs (Certificate)	28
Evans Evan	III	Boils on the leg	31
Archer John	IV	Weak lungs (Certificate) (Brompton Hos)	121
Smith Joseph	VI	Congestion of lungs (Ditto)	48
Barrett Edward	IV	Ring-worms on body	29
Gibbs George	II	Abscess following a chill	20
Strange James	IV	Heavy mass of timber fell on his head	20
Smith John	III	Gathering in the ear	12
Smith Thomas	III	Quinsy	20
Hollister Arthur (2)	III	Seized with fit in School	111
Judd Alfred	IV	Piece of glass cut his foot	18
Smith Charles	III	Part of hand cut off by a machine	18
Thompson Ernest (2)	IV	Internal disease again prostrated him	21
Batt Herbert	II	Inflammation of eyes with debility	35
Page Richard	IV	Rheumatism with slow fever	50
Hempton Walter	IV	Low Fever . . . . . Died 19. Sept.	30
Ball Herbert	II	Rheumatism with fever	52
Wilson Henry (2)	IV	Do in limbs	28
Thompson Ernt. (2)	IV	Internal disease	40
		Total absences because of sickness	2301

NB. The above particulars have been carefully collected from parents & School registers, & represent a true account.

∴ Average total = 302·4

∴ Average away ill = $\frac{2301}{302 \cdot 4}$ = 7·6 or 2·5 per cent.

This shows the numbers and causes of boys' absences from school in 1884-85.

Can you find out what all the diseases are?

Make a block chart showing the number of absences (half-days) for each reason.

You could group the reasons into accidents, fever, rheumatism, chest and lung sickness, internal (unknown), and so on.

Can you compare these figures with absences in your school?
You ought to choose the same number of boys. *Why?*

A School Inspector's log book

For a time, the amount of money paid to schools depended on how well the children knew their work when the Inspector called.

Summary of H.M. Inspector's Report dated 18th Augt 1891

Mixed School. The children are [or-] orderly and, although there have been three changes of Teachers during the year, have made satisfactory [pro-] progress. Reading is weak in the first standard; in the other standards it is good and intelligent. Spelling is somewhat weak. Arithmetic is on the whole satisfactory. Geography, taken as a Class Subject for the first time, is well-known. Needlework is fairly good. The Grant for Singing by Note cannot be recommended.

The first Standard is taught in a very dark classroom with no desks.

The South window in this room should be made larger and desks should be provided. The Registers must be tested by the Manager, at least once in each quarter at irregular intervals.

1891

82

Summary of H.M Inspector's
Report dated 18th Augt 1891
"Mixed School. The children are or--
derly and, although there have been
three changes of Teachers during the
year, have made satisfactory progress. Reading is weak in the first
Standard; in the other Standards it
is good and intelligent. Spelling is
somewhat weak. Arithmetic is on
the whole satisfactory. Geography,
taken as a Class subject for the first
time, is well known. Needlework is
fairly good. The Grant for Singing
by Note cannot be recommended
The first Standard is taught in
a very dark Class room with no desks
The South Window in this room
should be made larger and desks
should be provided. The Registers
must be tested by the Manager,
at least once in each quarter at
irregular intervals"

Were the children well behaved?
How many subjects does the Inspector mention?
Which one was so poor that no grant was going to be paid?
What did he find wrong with the school building?

Make up an Inspector's Report for your school.

The school curriculum

In this school log book it says how much time is to be spent on each subject. Some subjects had to be taught ('obligatory'). Compare this with your weekly lessons.

What is different? What is the same? Draw up a table like this and fill it in. Use a full page.

304

Time Table for Code 1882:–
Time allowed for each subject in hours:–

	Stan	I	II	III	IV	V–VII
Obligatory Subjects. –	Reading	5¼	5¼	4	4¾	4¼
	" History	.	.	1¼	1	1
	Writing	3¼	1½	1½	1	1
	Dictation	3½	3¼	3½	2¼	.
	Spelling	1½	1	1	1	.
	Composition	.	.	.	.	1¼
	Arithmetic	3½	4¾	4½	6¼	5
	Mental	1½	1	1	½	½
Optional Subjects. –	English Grammar	1	½	½	1	½
	Parsing	.	1¼	1¼	1	½
	Poetry	.	¼	½	½	½
	Analysis	.	.	.	.	½
	Geography	1	1	1	1½	1
	Map Drawing	.	½	½	¾	½
	Singing	¾	¾	¾	¾	¾
Specific Subjects. –	Algebra	.	.	.	.	1½
	Mechanics	.	.	.	.	1¼
Extra Subject. –	Drawing	.	.	.	.	1¼
		21¼	21¼	21¼	21¼	21¼

Summary of Time in hours

Stan	I	II	III	IV	V–VII
Obligatory Subjects	18½	16¾	16¾	15¾	13
Optional "	2¾	4½	4½	5½	4¼
Specific "	.	.	.	.	4
	21¼	21¼	21¼	21¼	21¼

School Songs taught & to be sung on day of Examination:–
First Division – Stan IV–VI:– Rounds:– "Good Night!" "The Bonnie Boat!" and "The Calender."

Lessons Taught	
Victorian Times	My School

Sewing

10

TEACHERS NOTES

VICTORIAN females needed to be skilled with the needle because they had to make their family's clothes and to hem sheets, tablecloths, and so on. Although men's jackets might be tailor-made, little else was. Many women earned money by sewing for richer families as well as their own. Clothes and household linen were commonly marked with the owner's name because, in most reasonably well-off households, washing was sent out to be done by a washerwoman. Poor people must have been perpetually surrounded by other people's wet washing.

The invention of the sewing machine was a real breakthrough. Isaac Singer, an American, did not patent his machine until 1850 and it was nearly ten years before the machine began to appear in Europe. In 1856, fast (aniline) dyes for printing all types of material were introduced and were immediately successful. Artificial silks were not produced commercially until the turn of the century.

GREAT REDUCTION IN PRICE.

ALWAYS THE BEST.

THEY ARE NOW THE CHEAPEST.

PRIZE MEDAL

ELASTIC STITCH AND LOCK STITCH SEWING MACHINES.

☞ Prospectus and Samples of Work sent free on application.—An inspection and comparison with all others is invited.

150, *REGENT STREET, LONDON, W.*, and 59, *BOLD STREET, LIVERPOOL.* [860

AGENT:—MISS M. DRAPER, BERLIN WAREHOUSE, 24, BENNETT'S HILL, BIRMINGHAM.

Victorian clothes

SEWING was expected to be done to a very high standard. Talk to the children about their own clothes. Where did they come from? Who made them? Are any handmade? Why did girls have to learn to sew so well? Did the Victorians buy ready-made clothes? Remind the children that there were no washing machines or driers, and no simple ways to heat water, which meant that people's clothes were not washed as often as they are today.

A sample piece of work like the apron illustrated (sheet 10A) would clearly have taken many hours to do. Discuss your children's estimates of the time it might have taken. Did they arrive at their estimates in a scientifically 'fair' way? Is it easy to make hand-sewn stitches all the same length? (The children could try for themselves.)

The numbered stitches (sheet 10A) are:

1. Hemming
2. Gathering
3. Buttonholes
4. Eyelet holes
5. Loops
6. Sewing on a button
7. Sewing on tapes
8. Pleats
9. Patch
10. Herringbone stitch

Making a sampler

First, the children should see a sampler. There are plenty of pictures available and reprinted patterns can be obtained from any shop dealing in embroidery and handcrafts but there is nothing like the real thing! The local museum may help but often the children will be your best source. Do take care, as they are valuable collectors' items.

Younger or less skilful children might design a sampler on paper. Otherwise they can complete the design on binca with fairly large stitches. For those with some skill or experience, try the following.

You will need:

2 mm squared paper
Ball-point pens, coloured pencils or crayons
Dressmaker's carbon
(Ordinary carbon will work but it is more messy.)
Calico or other fabric suitable for cross stitch
Sewing threads in lots of colours
(Pearlised cotton gives a nice shiny effect. Embroidery silks are fine but very fiddly.)
Pins

Begin by designing the sampler on the squared paper. So that this can be used for display or reference, photocopy it. Place the photocopy on top of a piece of carbon and pin both to the material (carbon dark-side down). On a firm surface, trace over the design with a ball-point pen. (The carbon can be re-used.) Unpin and start sewing, using colours to match the original design.

Here is an example of an 11-year old's work:

Stitching

Rose Cooper was born in 1870. When she was 11 years old, she made this strange little apron. She did not use a machine. The Victorians thought that it was important for girls to learn to sew. Rose Cooper made this at school to practise her stitching.

Try to match the correct numbers to each piece of work.

Here is what it shows:

____ Pleats

____ Patch

____ Sewing on a button

____ Loops

____ Hemming

____ Eyelet holes

____ Buttonholes

____ Herringbone stitch

____ Gathering

____ Sewing on tapes

R.E.Cooper
1881

1 2 3 4 5 6 7 8 9 10

If you had to do work like this at school, how long would it take you?
Work out a way to get an accurate estimate.

Making a sampler

Charlotte was only 7 years old when she made this sampler. It is sewn in cross stitch.

Design a sampler of your own on paper with small squares. Make a cross in coloured pencil to show each stitch.

You should include:

The alphabet
Your name and age
A text from the Bible or a saying like 'Never Tell Lies'
A border

You can now turn this design into a proper sampler.

DURING the nineteenth century, one child might have simple handmade toys or none at all, whilst another (sheet 11A) might have a full nursery. Poor children, when they were not working, played with improvised toys or home-made articles. Roy's parents were clearly able to indulge their children and to purchase from the enormous range of toys available. Most of the toys came from abroad, particularly Germany and France. Humming tops, board games, strong wooden toys, and miniature tea services were made in Britain. British toy shops were famous for the variety of goods that they sold and British toy-makers gradually took more of the market. 'Brittains' began making their lead soldiers in the 1890s. (Lead is now banned from children's toys.) Meccano was invented at the turn of the century by Frank Hornby.

AN interesting science topic can be developed from a toy survey. You can investigate safety, durability, and play value. Involve the children in devising fair tests. Send your results to the local newspaper or community newsletter.

Simply research Victorian Toys. Look in books and magazines, in the cupboards at home and in museums. The children can be encouraged to talk to elderly people for their memories of childhood. These will not be Victorian but could still provide some useful material.

As well as the toys in sheets 11B and 11C, you might try making an Aunt Sally, bean bags, a peep show, a jumping jack or a jack-in-the-box. Hoop games in the playground or blowing bubbles from clay pipes take little preparation.

Make two dolls' houses out of boxes, one rich and one poor. Work from evidence; have the children do some simple research.

How did people amuse themselves before television? The children could learn some country dances or popular Victorian songs. Have a concert where everyone does a 'turn'. Be inventive: anything is permissible, from reciting parlour poems to fire-eating (pretend fire, of course, using tissue torches and lots of showmanship).

Nursery toys

A boy called Roy wrote this. The whole list actually took two pages.

> Roy has a bank of England pencil and so has Maud both of them has got a little Indian rubber. Roy has got a lot of pens Maud has only got a few. Maud has got from twenty five to thirty dolls and Roy has got nearly twenty boxes of soldiers with three hundred and thirty soldiers. Maud has got a lovely theatre Roy has a fly that flys along Maud has a large dolls house Roy has a pair of horses you can drive. Maud and Roy has a nice pair of reins . . . Maud has nine or ten doll sets of chairs and tables and Roy has nine or ten boxes of bricks. Roy is fonder of soldiers little fish to swim precious stones coins and puppys that go along. Maud is fonder of dolls and chiner tea sets. Roy and Maud have threepence a week.

Make a list of your toys. Compare it with Roy's or Maud's toys.
Do you have any of the toys on their list?
Did you make as many mistakes as Roy when you wrote your list?

Home-made toys: a thaumatrope

Can you see an object that is out of sight? Make this popular Victorian toy and you will see . . . *or will you?*

- Cut out a circle, about 6 cm across, from stiff card. (You can draw round a cup or a jar.)
- Make two holes at the edge of the circle, as shown here.
- Cut two pieces of string about 15 cm long. Tie a knot in one end of each. Thread one string through each hole. One knot should be on the front of the card, the other on the back.
- Draw the two pictures, as shown here. Colour them. This example is of a parrot and a cage.
- Hold the strings tight in both hands. Twist the strings between fingers and thumb to make the circle spin.
- What happens?

You could make your own drawings. Remember that half of the drawing goes on one side and half on the other.

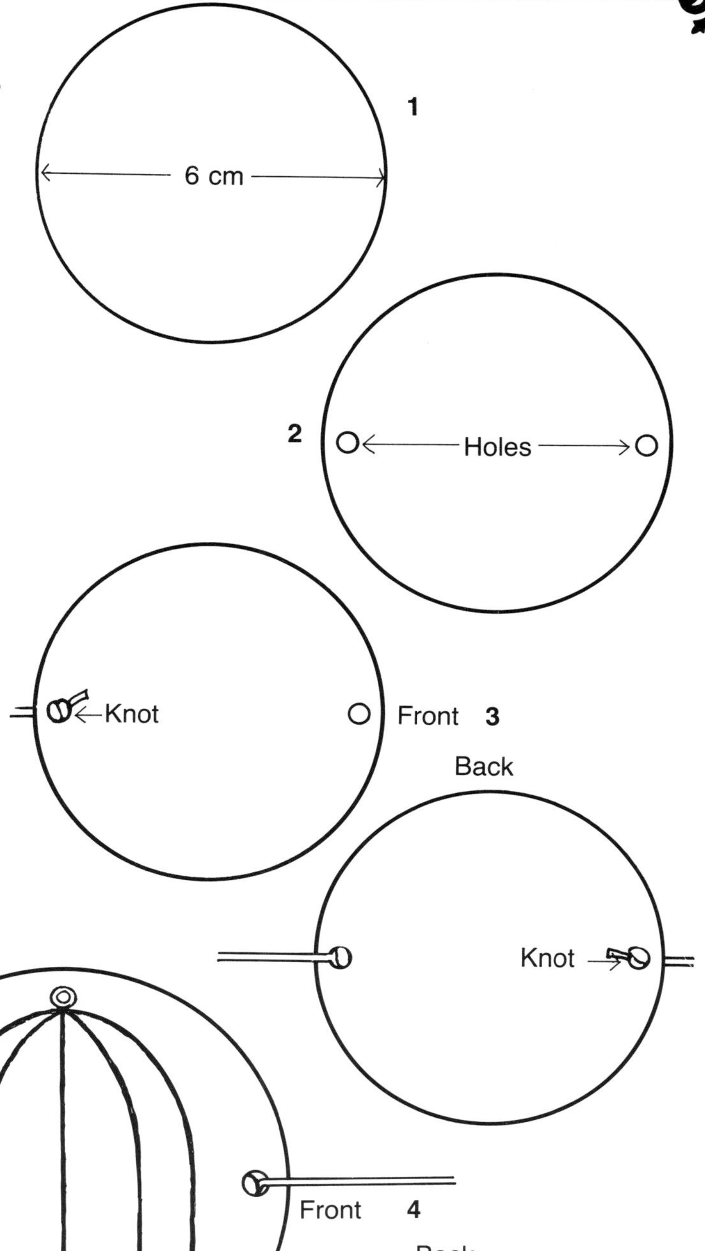

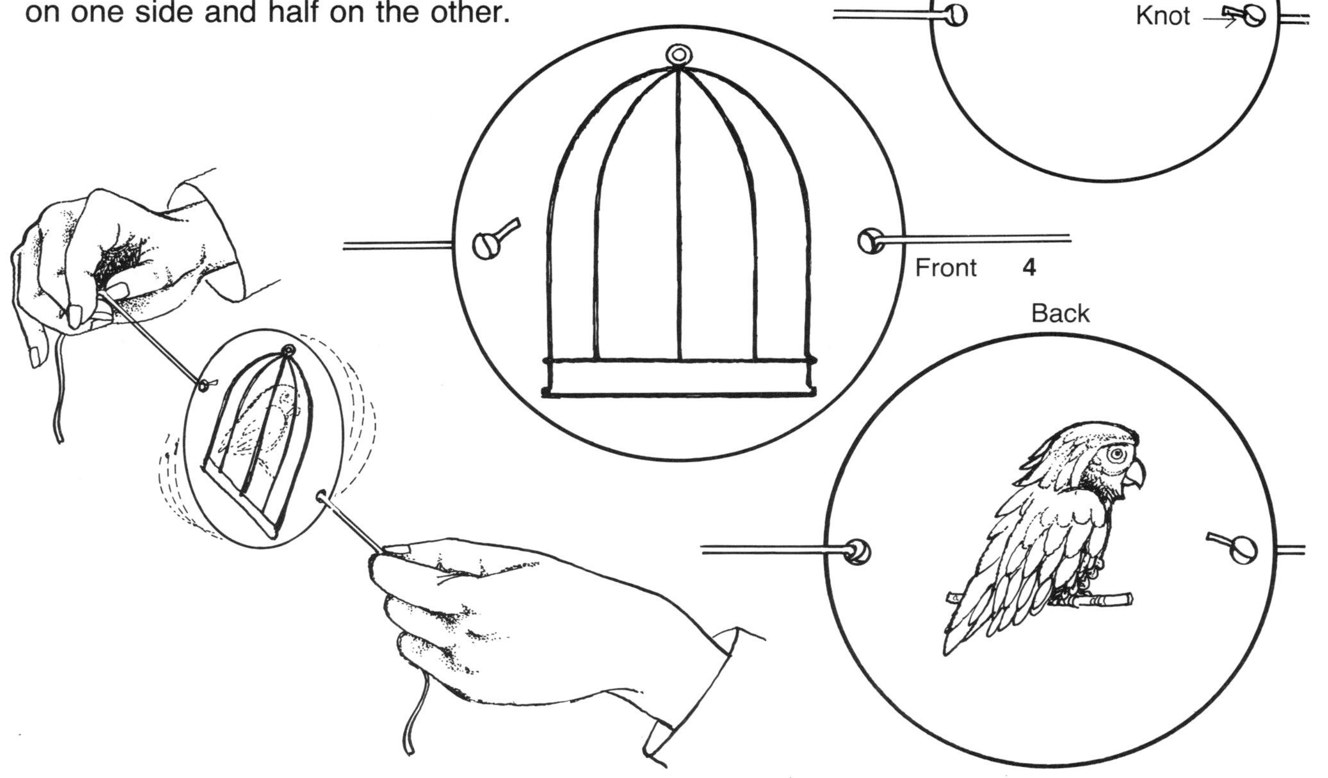

Home-made toys: a peg doll

To make a peg doll you will need:

A dolly peg
A pipe cleaner
Oddments of material, scraps of lace
Scissors
Needle and thread
Pins

The Victorians used to make some of their peg dolls into pedlar dolls, like the one on the right. To do this you would need some ribbons and some strings of buttons. What else could you add for her to sell?

1 Cut out two pieces of fabric for the sleeves (each 10 × 4 cm).

2 Cut out one piece for the skirt (12.5 × 11 cm).

3 Wind the middle of the pipe cleaner around the neck of the peg and twist firmly at the back. Spread the ends – the arms – sideways. Bend the points under to make 'hands'.

4 Press in 5 cm along one long side and both short sides of the sleeve pieces and lay them right sides facing.
Sew both long edges together from the left and right, leaving a hole in the middle of each edge for the head and body.
Turn the sleeves the right way out and fit on to the peg, putting the head of the peg through the hole and the pipe cleaner through the arms.

5 Place the shorter edges of the skirt together with the right sides facing.

6 Back-stitch along it.

7 Turn up the bottom edge.

8 Turn the right side out and decorate with lace.

9 Gather the top of the skirt and attach it to the bottom of the sleeve part.

10 Draw a face and glue on some wool for hair. Add a hat.

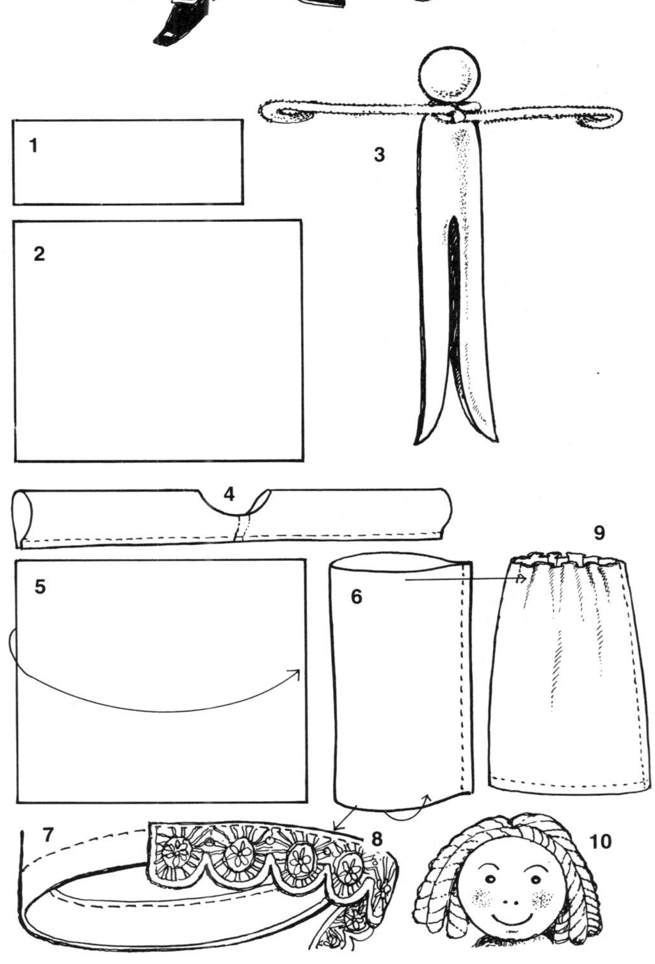

THE Victorian era was a boom time for the building industry. The demand for homes and factories, as well as public buildings, hospitals, and so on, was enormous.

VICTORIAN buildings make excellent subjects for observational art.

Make line drawings of a town hall or a school building and enhance them by the use of coloured ink washes (*Brusho*[1] or similar). Fine black fibre-tipped pens or even ball-point pens make an interesting change from 2B pencils. Experiment first with the ink washes before letting children loose on the sketches.

Compile a Victorian folio by sketching building details (windows, doors, guttering, chimneys).

A model (a town house, terraced row, rectory, school, etc.) is a worthwhile co-operative exercise. (National Curriculum attainment targets again.) Take or obtain photographs and measurements and then work to scale. How can you work out the height of the building? What scale should you use? Have the children tackle these questions orally, perhaps in groups at first. Build in a realistic way, using as much detail as possible. Roof struts, individual tiles, and surrounding walls can be included. Use *Mod-Roc*[2] to give the walls texture and extra strength.

Carry out a building survey. Check every detail of a Victorian school, rectory, town hall or other accessible building. Where are the windows? toilets? heating systems? Devise a report sheet, check list or information matrix that can be used to compare an old building with a new one (see sheet 12A).

('Cob', as listed in the materials section of 12A, is a mixture of clay, gravel and straw).

Devising a cartoon

Health regulations took a little time to catch up with the rapid rate of building construction. Services were often stretched to breaking point. The children might enjoy devising their own version of a cartoon of 1849 which suggested a way of avoiding the smell from broken and overworked sewers. ('Gutta Percha' was similar to rubber.) This might balance the rather romantic view of the street given in sheet 12B.

NEW USE FOR GUTTA PERCHA.

IN addition to drinking-cups, driving-bands, whips, hats, splints, portable soup, shoes, elastic heads, coats, candles, tubing, tenpenny nails, theatrical banquets, picture-frames, saveloys, buttons, baskets, biscuits, and other various forms into which that universal material Gutta Percha has been converted, we beg to suggest a new and sanitary employment from this multiform substance, to which its connexion with the gutter would seem naturally to adapt it.

We would suggest that masks with pipes of Gutta Percha might be employed in London and other large towns, for enabling the wearer to breathe the upper and purer currents of air, in the neighbourhood of our slaughter-houses, cattle markets, graveyards, bone-boilers', soap-makers', and cat-gut manufacturers'. Without some such arrangement we do not see how the Londoner is to enjoy the "sweet airs that give delight and hurt not" which we are assured by philosophers *do* exist somewhere above our heads, and of which we may be allowed to breathe the name, if we cannot breathe any more substantial part of them.

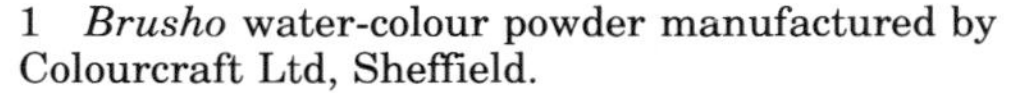

1 *Brusho* water-colour powder manufactured by Colourcraft Ltd, Sheffield.
2 *Mod-Roc* fabric reinforced plaster made by T.J. Smith & Nephew Ltd, Welwyn Garden City and Hull.

A building record sheet

Victorian record sheet

Record the details of a building near you on this sheet. Choose one that you think might be Victorian. It is not always easy to tell, since buildings do have rooms added from time to time. Survey your own house and compare the two.

Include a photograph or drawing of the building with this record sheet.

Type of building ______________________

Name/address ______________________

____

____

Number of storeys ______________________

(Tick) Detached ☐ Semi-detached ☐

Terraced ☐ Other ______________________

Sketch of building plan:

DRAW ON SEPARATE SHEET

Direction faced by main entrance ______________________

Materials used for the outside:

(Tick) Wall ☐ Brick ☐ Stone ☐

Rendering ☐ Timber frame ☐

Tile hanging ☐ Cob ☐ Chalk ☐

Other ______________________

Type of water supply ______________________

Was there a well? ______________________

Materials used for chimneys ______________________

____

Sketch type of window:

Inside (if you are allowed in)

(Tick) Internal doors: Planks ☐ Panels ☐

Other ______________________

Are the doors flat? ______________________

Internal walls are made of ______________________

____

Number of fireplaces: ______________________

Size of largest: ______________________

Other obvious features (e.g. beams, date stone): ______________________

____

When was the house built? (Estimate if necessary but try to give reasons.) ______________________

____

In the street

This drawing was made in 1845. It shows some of the people in a busy street between six and seven o'clock on a summer's morning. *Who are these people? Can you spot the milk seller and the plasterer in the top row?*

Make up short stories about some of the people. Say who they are, what they do for a living and why they are up so early in the morning.

Apprentices

One way of learning a trade in Victorian times was to become an apprentice. Here is part of an agreement (Indenture) between Arthur Watts and William Pratt, which made young Arthur into Mr Pratt's apprentice. All of the underlined words were handwritten in the actual Indenture.

PRATT'S SADDLER'S BUSINESS
Premises: The thatched cottage
adjoining Mr Perry's Shop, Avebury

This Indenture, made the <u>thirteenth</u> day of <u>June,</u> One thousand eight hundred and seventy eight, between <u>Arthur John William Watts (a Minor) Son of Sarah Ann Appleton of Marlborough in the County of Wilts Widow</u> . . . <u>of the one part and William Chapman Pratt of Avebury</u> . . . <u>Saddler of the other part</u>.

. . . <u>Arthur John William Watts</u> . . . doth . . . put, place and bind himself Apprentice to the said <u>William Chapman Pratt</u> . . . to serve from the day of the date hereof, for and until the full end and term of <u>seven</u> years . . . [He] shall, during such term, faithfully serve his said Master, his secrets keep, his lawful commands everywhere gladly do; . . . he shall do no damage to his said Master, nor see any done by others; . . . he shall not waste the goods of his said Master, nor lend them unlawfully to others; . . . nor without the license or consent of his said Master, shall he buy or sell, haunt taverns or playhouses, or absent himself from his Master's service day or night unlawfully, but shall in all things act as a faithful Apprentice; . . . he shall give a true and just account of his said Master's goods, chattels and money committed to his charge. . . .

The said <u>William Chapman Pratt</u> . . . will, by the best means that he can, teach and instruct . . . the said <u>Arthur John William Watts</u> in the Art, Trade or Business of a <u>Saddler</u> . . . and will allow and pay to his Apprentice weekly . . . the following wages: for the second year of the said term <u>one</u> shilling, for the third year <u>two</u> shillings, for the fourth year <u>three</u> shillings, for the fifth year <u>four</u> shillings, for the sixth year <u>five</u> shillings, and for the seventh year <u>six</u> shillings.

This Indenture, made the Thirteenth day of June, One thousand eight hundred and seventy eight Between Arthur John William Watts a Minor Son of Sarah Ann Appleton [illegible] of Marlborough in the County of Wilts Widow and the said Sarah Ann [illegible] Appleton of the one part and William Chapman Pratt of Avebury in the said County of Wilts Saddler of the other part

Witnesseth, that the said Arthur John William Watts, with the consent and approbation of the said Sarah Ann [illegible] Appleton, doth by these presents put, place, and bind himself Apprentice to the said William Chapman Pratt to learn his Art, Trade, or Business of a Saddler, as hereinafter mentioned, with him (after the manner of an Apprentice), to serve from the day of the date hereof, for and unto the full end and term of [illegible] Years, from hence next following, and fully to be complete and ended. And the said Sarah Ann Appleton doth hereby for [illegible] heirs, executors, and administrators, covenant with the said William Chapman Pratt, his executors and administrators, that the said Arthur John William Watts shall, [illegible] serve his said Master, his secrets keep, his lawful commands everywhere gladly do; that he shall [illegible] to his said Master, nor see [illegible] shall forth[illegible] to his said Master [illegible]

What was William Pratt's trade?
What must Mr Pratt do for Arthur?
What must Arthur do in return?

Make an Indenture with your name on it. Use some of the words given here. Make it look as real as you can. Use pen and ink to write in the names and so on.
What trade will you be apprentice to?
What sort of rules will you have to obey?

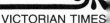

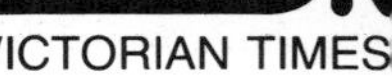

Church restoration

ONE of the most striking differences between the Victorian age and our own was the amount of visible religious observance. On 30 March 1851, we know from an official survey that over 7 million people attended church (population 18 million), about 60 per cent of the eligible population. Attendance in rural areas, where the gentry were not averse to keeping registers of attendance, was higher than in towns, where the bulk of absentees came from the working classes.

The Victorians lavished care and attention on their churches. Over half of parish churches were restored. The Victorians were also the greatest builders of new churches since the Normans. Today, even in buildings that are predominantly medieval, what greets us inside is a Victorian vision of how a church should be.

Victorian architecture remains largely out of favour. Of the many listed buildings in the Manchester and Salford area, for example, not one is a Victorian church. Many were pulled down during slum clearance; many are disused and, as they become dangerous, are being demolished, usually without opposition.

John Betjeman was, of course, a great champion of Victorian architecture.

THE poem (sheet 13A) was written to fit the metre of a well-known Anglican hymn, hence the title ('The Church's One Foundation', hymn 255 in *Hymns Ancient and Modern*, tune 'Aurelia' by S.S. Wesley). The children should realise that the poem can be sung. Why was it made to fit a hymn tune?

Writing to a known tune pattern is a useful device for helping children to write poetry. They could use the idea, although not necessarily the tune, that was used by Betjeman. Write in praise (or otherwise) of the building of the school. Alternatively, re-fight Victorian arguments over the building of the railways or of the Crystal Palace (see pp 83–6).

Organise a 'before and after' project

The main features of a church – altar, pews, pulpit, etc. – need to be known for this exercise, so a preparatory visit to a local church is desirable. If the church contains Victorian work, prepare an outline plan and let the children mark down the Victorian additions. Apart from the opportunities that a visit provides for model-making and for observational art, you may be able to get ideas for making stained glass windows or tiles (see page 80).

Prepare (or ask an artistic colleague to do so!) two large and uncluttered drawings of the interior of a village church in the mid-nineteenth century. The first picture should be an impression of the interior before extensive Victorian restoration, looking either towards the altar or from above. Some disrepair should be evident: plaster cracks, uneven floor, leaky roof. Include high box pews perhaps a little awry, ornate Jacobean altar rail, plain window panes, medieval-style roof beams, small altar, and a trace of wall paintings. (All of these features should be labelled.) The second picture should show the bare bones of the same interior (empty floors, no pews, no window panes, no altar or rails, no pulpit, no roof) for the children to complete as it appeared after restoration. There must be room for the children to add the stained glass windows, etc.

Ask the children to pretend that they are a Victorian church architect who is given the task of restoration. They must complete the second picture in colour, showing the changes that they have made. (The poem will help them.) They could also write a brief architect's report for the Churchwardens, describing what they have done.

Plan a campaign

Have the children plan a full-scale campaign to save a local Victorian church (or alternative building) from demolition. Organise meetings and debates; write letters to the newspapers; improvise television interviews; paint posters and banners.

RE follow-up work

Look at the religious functions of various parts of the church. Why is the font where it is? (You could re-enact a christening service and have a party afterwards.) What is the altar used for? Try examining some Victorian hymns. Simply counting how many there are in a standard hymn book is revealing. Why is the language so difficult?

For a different perspective, examine the Salvation Army and Victorian social problems. Lively Salvationist rhythms, tambourines and tassels also contrast strongly with John Betjeman's 'Hymn'. Teach a tambourine routine to a group of children; the School Concert will never be quite the same again!

Reading

Further insights on Betjeman and this particular subject can be gained from reading his introduction to *English Parish Churches*, Collins 1958, or *The Best of Betjeman*, Penguin 1978.

St Mary's Cathedral, Glasgow.

Restoration of a church

This poem describes the way in which Victorian architects repaired and altered old churches. Read it carefully.

The Church's Restoration
In eighteen-eighty-three
Has left for contemplation
Not what there used to be.
How well the ancient woodwork
Looks round the Rect'ry hall,
Memorial of the good work
Of him who plann'd it all.

He who took down the pew-ends
And sold them anywhere
But kindly spared a few ends
Work'd up into a chair.
O worthy persecution
Of dust! O hue divine!
O cheerful substitution,
Thou varnishéd pitch-pine!

Church furnishing! Church furnishing!
Sing art and crafty praise!
He gave the brass for burnishing
He gave the thick red baize,
He gave the new addition,
Pull'd down the dull old aisle,
– To pave the sweet transition
He gave th' encaustic tile.

Of marble brown and veinéd
He did the pulpit make;
He order'd windows stainéd
Light red and crimson lake.
Sing on, with hymns uproarious,
Ye humble and aloof,
Look up! and oh how glorious
He has restored the roof!

John Betjeman

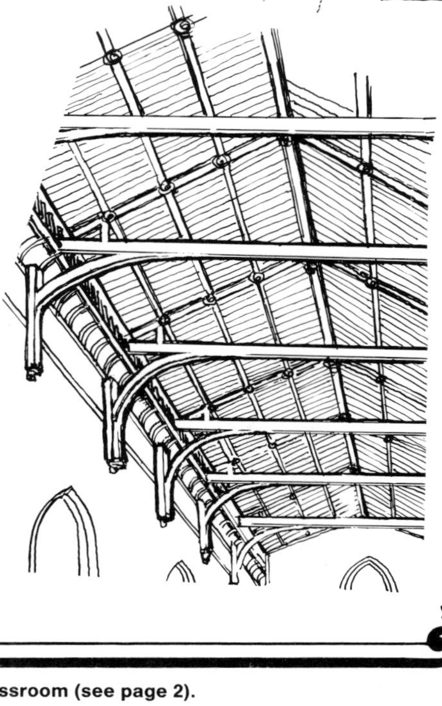

Do you think the poet approved of the work?
How can you tell?
Underline all of the words that tell you what changes were made.

Victorian tiles

ENGLISH tile-making was all but dead at the start of the nineteenth century. Its processes and skills had to be re-invented by the Victorians. The encaustic (inlaid) tile was revived in the late 1830s by Herbert Minton. He stamped an impression into thick red clay and poured in liquid white clay. It sounds easy but there were technical problems which Minton took time to overcome. He made a decorative pavement at Osborne House for Prince Albert in 1844 and later paved the corridors of Westminster. Inlaid tiles were also used in churches.

A housing boom during the last decades of the century, coupled with a tightening-up of building and health standards, encouraged mass production. Halls, bathrooms, and fireplaces were all liable to tessellation. Tiles even appeared on furniture, on wash stands and sideboards. For reasons of good hygiene, hospitals, butchers' and fishmongers' shops were tiled.

The Victorians happily copied their designs from the Greeks, the Romans, or the Far East, with flowers the most repeated motif. Most tiles which were mass-produced at the end of the century were decorated by transfer printing from an engraved metal plate. Some big panels were hand-painted, however.

Arts and crafts

MAKE an inlaid tile. Roll out a slab of clay and cut out a 6″ × 6″ square. Some types of clay are more suitable for tile-making than others, which resist staying flat, so seek advice from your supplier. Have the children scale up one of the designs (practical maths) on sheet 14A or invent their own, then prick or copy the design on to clay, and incise. The depression should then be filled with slip (liquid clay) of a different colour. Leave to dry slowly on a flat surface, then fire and clear-glaze or varnish. There are other ways of producing the design on clay. It can be painted on to a glazed tile, using on-glaze paints. Alternatively, the design can be coloured before glazing. It depends on the materials available.

Older juniors can do lino cutting, using the correct tools, under careful supervision. Depending on how it is cut, a negative or positive print can be made in the lino. This should be mounted on a block of wood. When printed on to fabric, using fabric inks, cushion covers, table-cloths, etc. can be produced.

A safe and simple printing block can be made using felt or string stuck on to a block. Dilute PVA adhesive (Marvin Medium or similar) is a good way of adding a gloss to the resulting prints. The wall panel (sheet 14B) can be made as a co-operative exercise in this way. Should you make a shop front, ensure that the words are comprised of letters of the same style. This can be difficult, so cheat by using a computer program (e.g. PenDown Signwriter). Turn the corner of the classroom into a Victorian shop or hallway; it can be very effective (see sheet 14B).

Mathematics

Tiles make a great starting-point for doing mathematics. Investigate the axes of symmetry of the designs. Why are most tiles square? Could they be pentagonal? Weigh a tile. How much do all the tiles in a bathroom weigh? A good maths scheme (e.g. Nuffield) will provide you with plenty of ideas on tessellations and symmetry. Victorian wallpapers are quite fashionable, so it is easy to obtain a range of patterns to work with.

Visits

Gladstone Pottery Museum, Uttoxeter Road, Longton, Stoke-on-Trent. (0782) 31922
Ironbridge Gorge Museum, Shropshire. (095 245) 3522
People's Palace Museum, Glasgow Green, Glasgow. (041) 554 0233

Tile designs

These are Victorian tiles.

Are all of the patterns symmetrical?
Can you mark in all *the axes of symmetry?*

Use a ruler marked in inches (just as the Victorians would have done) to measure them. Victorian tiles were 6 inches square.
What do you notice about the size of these tiles?

Tile panels

These Victorian tiled panels are in different places. One is on a butcher's shop, the other in a hospital ward for children.
What are they for?

Inside, the butcher's shop is tiled floor to ceiling.
Why?

Design a tiled panel of your own.
Where would you use it?

Watch out, there are tiles about!
Can you find any – around front doors and the porches of old houses, inside old houses, shops, etc?

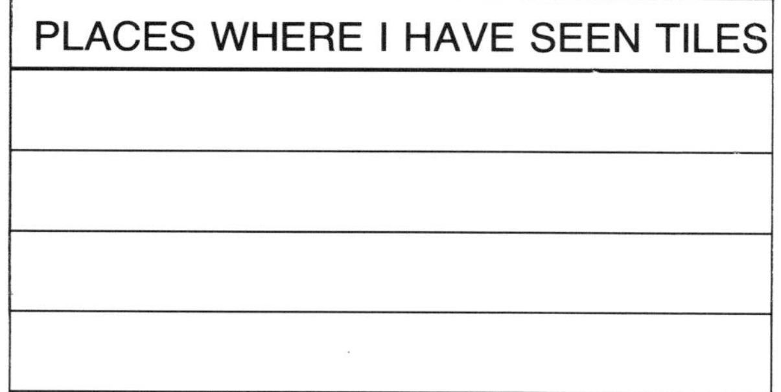

PLACES WHERE I HAVE SEEN TILES

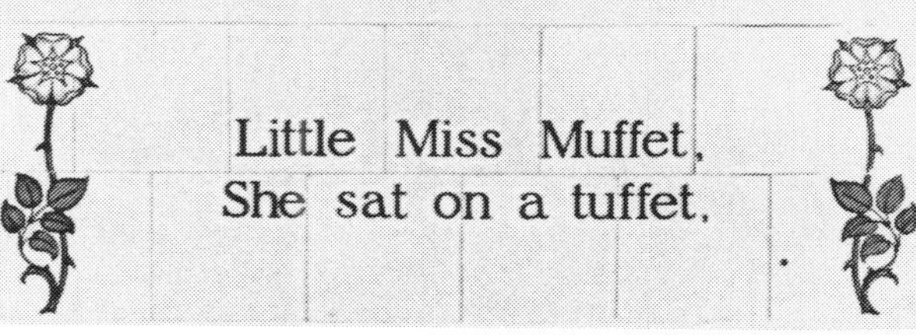

Tiles on the wards

Fifty five large tiled panels decorate four childrens' wards at the Royal Victoria Hospital, Newcastle upon Tyne. This is the country's finest collection of Victorian tile-pictures.

The panels were ordered for the hospital in the late 19th century. Today the nursery rhyme pictures help to cheer up the patients and are often the topic of conversation among visitors.

The Great Exhibition 1851

15

TEACHERS NOTES

SUCH was the success of the Great Exhibition in 1851 that even the public toilets made a profit. Success did not seem likely when the idea was originally conceived. There was apathy as well as outright opposition. However, Prince Albert provided the support necessary to sustain the venture, and a civil servant, Henry Cole, provided the organisation. Queen Victoria donated £1000 towards the funding of the project, which was done by public subscription.

The Great Exhibition was about industrial progress, trade, and patriotism. Contemporaries stressed its themes of Progress, Work, Religion, and Peace. Technological advances, such as Trevithick's steam engine (1801) and Nasmyth's steam hammer (1839), had made mass production speedier and cheaper, so that it was possible to make everyday objects very decorative. The Victorians delighted in the new-found facility to ornament things. They had confidence that an exhibition would show the superioriy of British design but there was also much reflection about the quality of French design.

A competition to design the exhibition building attracted 233 entries. Light had to come from the roof, and the building had to be made of fire-proof materials. Joseph Paxton's winning design used cast-iron and glass. It had to be redesigned, by public demand, to enclose three giant elms. Conservationist pressure is clearly nothing new. The building was erected in Hyde Park within six months. (In 1852 it was dismantled and moved to Sydenham – the area of London now known as Crystal Palace.)

FACTFILE

The building was 1848 ft long (over three times that of St Paul's Cathedral), 408 ft wide, and covered 19 acres. Its highest point was 108 ft. Nearly every measurement in the building was a multiple of 24. It contained 202 miles of iron sash bars, 24 miles of gutters, and 293 655 panes of glass. The interior colour scheme was red, light blue, yellow and white. (Vertical surfaces were blue.)

There were over 100 000 exhibits. Price labels were not allowed. The exhibition had over six million visitors in five months. The greatest number in the building at one time was 93 224. Visitors consumed nearly 2 million buns and 1 million bottles of lemonade. 270 gallons of Eau de Cologne and other scents were given away free and well over 600 lbs of chocolate drops were tasted on various displays. The profit of £186,000 was enough to purchase the South Kensington museum sites.

Dissected puzzles

THE picture (sheet 15A) can be mounted on card, and turned into a facsimile Victorian puzzle. Colouring should be as realistic as possible. 'Dissecting puzzles' were invented at the end of the eighteenth century as educational tools. They mostly featured moral or religious subjects. The children could try making their own. What pictures do they think would be suitable? Collect illustrations and make a class set of dissected puzzles, which are of course easier to make than jigsaws. Plywood and mechanised cutting tools did not make the true tongued jigsaws cheaply available until the end of the Victorian period.

Sheet 15A could also be made into an OHP transparency. Photocopiers will do this.

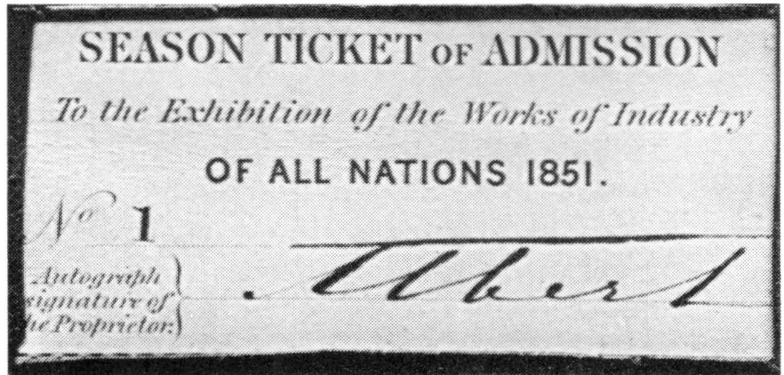

Hold a competition

Let the children design their own Crystal Palace, working in two or three dimensions. Sheet 15B shows an ingenious glazing wagon which kept the glaziers dry in wet weather. This is just one clever solution to one of the tricky building problems faced in 1851. Pose some problems for the class to investigate. Troops tramping in step tested a section of gallery. Let the children devise some tests of their own. How would they have coped with the problem of condensation running off the glass? (Gutters were so designed as to have channels inside and out.) Some objections were raised to the chopping down of elm trees in Hyde Park. What solution to this problem can the children come up with? (The building was erected over some of them. Sparrowhawks were employed to get rid of the sparrows.)

Find out where the exhibits came from

Obtain from the V & A a copy of the ground plan of the building which shows how the exhibition space was allocated. Simplify the plan if necessary to suit your class. Have them make an alphabetical list of all the countries named on the plan. Are there any names that they do not recognise? They can check their list in an atlas. Can they find them all? Which continent do most of them come from? Why do the children think this is? What goods did each country put on display? Can the children find out from the plan? You could also use the plan as a basis for model-building.

Relive the past

The process of planning and putting on the Great Exhibition can be relived through role play, drama, debates, writing, art and craft. You could start by putting up posters inviting children to a public meeting to discuss the idea. An adult could attend as Prince Albert to explain the reasons and the problems. A little imagination and acting in role is needed. The children might then tackle some of the real problems of the project. Where should it be sited? Examine a nineteenth-century OS map of London for a site of about 20 acres. (David & Charles publish four maps – numbers 71, 72, 79 and 80 – which cover the London area.) Organise a Parliamentary debate to argue over the choice of site. Which building design is to be chosen? Who is to be invited to exhibit? The children could write letters to manufacturers, and design tickets and a museum logo. Many poems and popular songs were composed about the Exhibition. The children could try doing this.

An exhibition day could be set up in the school hall. There could be a stained glass gallery, ornate chairs (school chairs with added corrugated card), machines with giant cogwheels, and so on. Medals could be awarded to the best exhibitors. Refreshments – small sandwiches, soft drinks and bath buns – could be served. Remember, neither smoking nor alcohol was allowed, and dogs were not permitted either.

A follow-up discussion could focus on the benefits or otherwise of the Great Exhibition. Was it 'The Great Humbug of 1851'?

Design

Sheet 15C could be followed up in detail but you must judge how far you can go with your particular children. Classroom displays of craftsmen-made and machine-made objects might grow progressively. 'Good design' and 'bad design' tables would provide the starting-point for discussion, drawing, design and technology. Let the children bring objects for display. Should design suit the material? Can styles be mixed together in one piece? Is function everything? What is bad taste?

The Crystal Palace: a dissected puzzle 15A

Crystal Palace is a football team. It is also a place in London where a huge building once stood. The iron and glass building, called the Crystal Palace, was first erected in Hyde Park for the Great Exhibition in 1851.

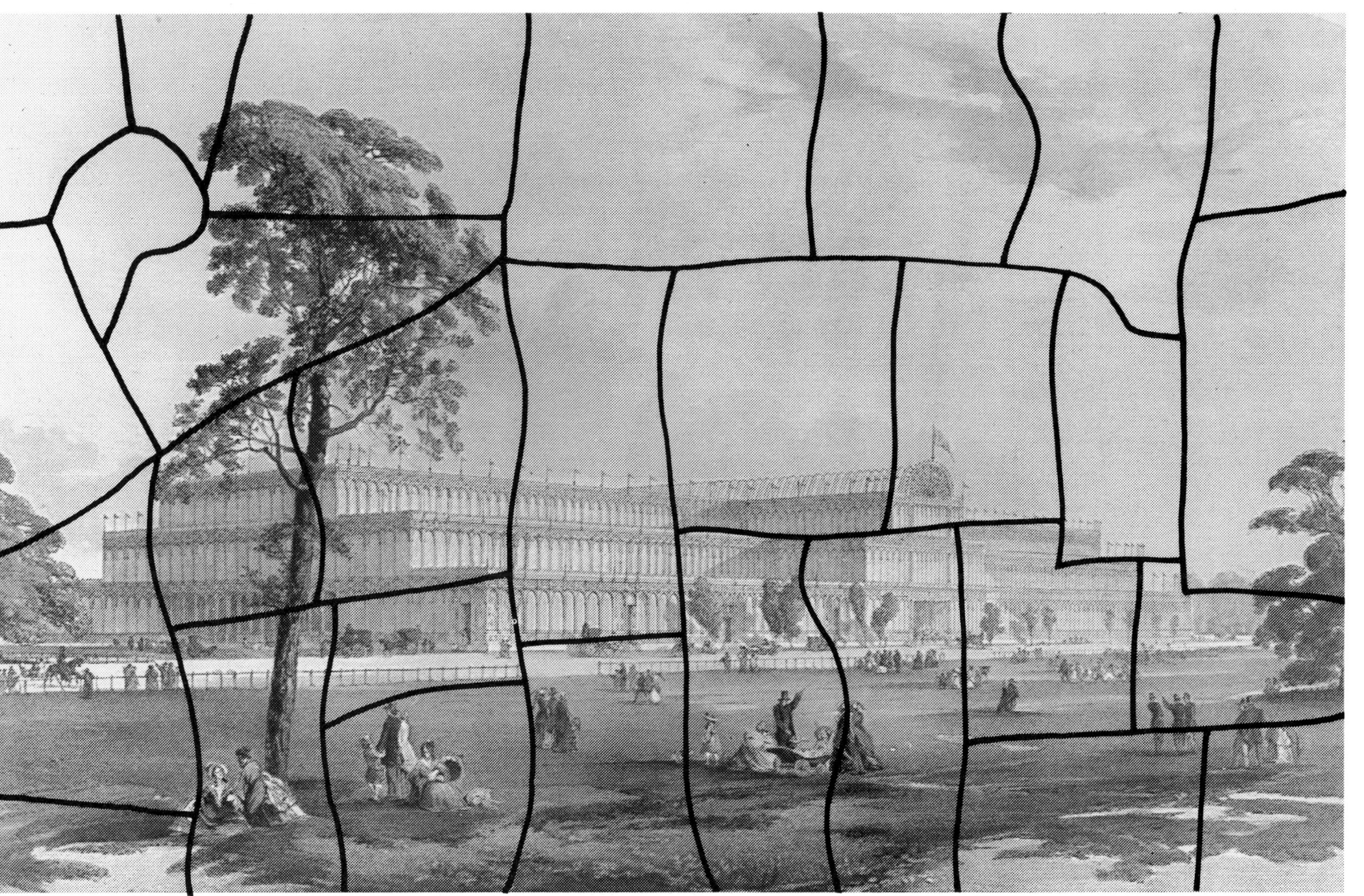

The Crystal Palace building

There was a competition to design the building. This was the winning design. *What sort of building would you design for a Great Exhibition?*

The light had to come from the roof. *Why?*

Examine these drawings, made at the time.

What do they tell you about the building of the Crystal Palace?

A clever tool: a glazing waggon

Troops testing a sample section of gallery

The Great Exhibition: some exhibits

Here are a few of the thousands of exhibits.

*Can you match the labels **1–5** to the objects **A–E** ?*

1 From Canada, a black walnut 'Tete-à-tete'
2 From Britain, a fish knife and fork
3 From Britain, a sportsman's knife
4 From Ireland, a table
5 From Prussia (Germany), a stove of polished iron plate

Write catalogue entries for some of these exhibits. Include what the product is made of, how it should be used, and all of its wonderful advantages.

A

C

E

B

D

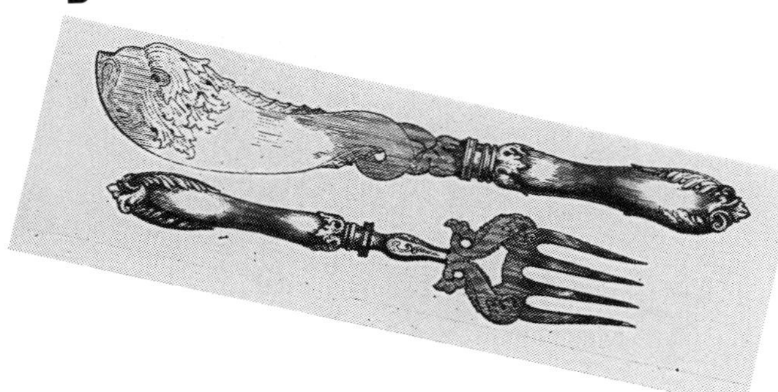

Here are two descriptions from the official catalogue.

Ventilating Hats
'. . . A series of channels is cut in thin cork which is fastened to the leather lining, and a valve fixed at the top may be opened and shut at pleasure, allowing the perspiration to escape.'

The Registered Alarum Bedstead
'. . . Immediately the alarum ceases ringing, the front legs are made to fold underneath, and the sleeper, without any jerk or slightest personal danger, is placed upon his feet in the middle of the room, where a cold bath may be placed to ensure being rendered rapidly wide awake.'

Try drawing the hat and bedstead in action. Follow the descriptions.

Railways

RAILWAYS were a big Victorian success story. They probably had more impact on the lives of ordinary people than any other development. The railways grew at an astonishing speed. In the 1840s, building railways became a mania and fortunes were easily made and just as easily lost.

Railways were highly visible. Gangs of unruly navvies invaded quiet rural communities: building bridges, digging cuttings, excavating tunnels, and generally disturbing the locals.

Economically the impact of railways was obvious. Industries expanded, especially coal and steel, and goods became cheaper. This in turn affected employment opportunities and there was demand, both at home and abroad, for the skills needed in railway construction. Wider markets were opened to all producers; even agriculture benefited as a result. Ports expanded to cope with the extra trade. Fishing ports also flourished. Speedy distribution meant that goods became increasingly standardised and branded names became familiar nationally. A number of traditional crafts did suffer, and canal and coach companies were put out of business. However, the mail was speeded, newspapers gained national audiences, and politicians were able to campaign with ease across the country. People were able to travel to the seaside, or to the Great Exhibition. The journey from Liverpool to London now took six and a half hours instead of the previous twenty-four. With improved transport, suburbs grew apace.

LET the children pretend to be local farmers threatened by the passage of the railway. Write letters to the press stating objections to the development.

Design a holiday poster encouraging people to visit the seaside by train. What resorts did people favour? What did the trains look like?

Make a tape recording of a busy Victorian railway terminus. What sort of sounds would you hear? Make up the conversations of travellers waiting to board trains. The W.P. Frith picture, 'The Railway Station', (1862) would be a good stimulus to this activity.

Research and prepare interviews with famous men (such as Richard Trevithick, George Stephenson, Isambard Brunel, George Hudson) involved in the development of the railways. This work could be a group project, written or recorded, acted out in costume for a class assembly, or produced and performed as a television broadcast (a mini *Question Time* or *This is Your Life*).

THE GROWTH OF BRITAIN'S RAILWAYS

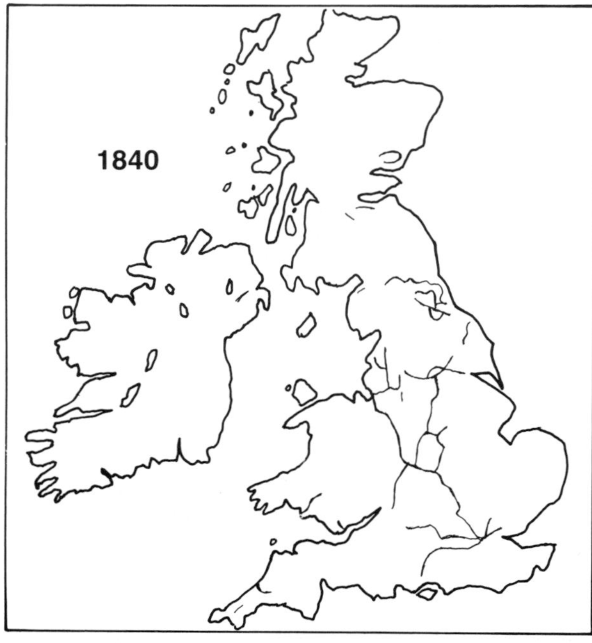

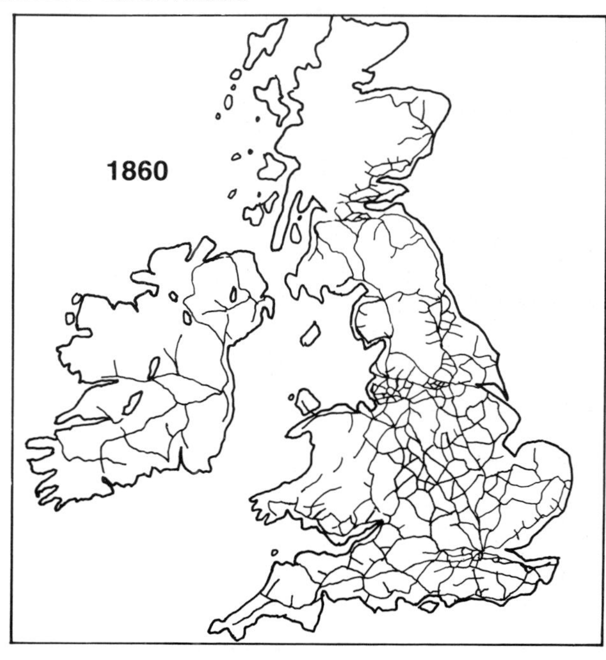

Railways: planning a route

The world's first covered railway station was built at Temple Meads, Bristol in 1840. It was at one end of a line that was to stretch from London to Bristol.

Imagine that you are the engineer responsible for deciding where this line is to go. Here are your orders:

1 The line must go as straight as possible to avoid curves that will slow the train.

2 There must be no steep hills and as few tunnels as possible because they are expensive.

3 Reading and Bath must be on the line because that will be good for business.

4 Land owned by important people must be avoided as much as possible. They might cause trouble by objecting.

Plan your route on this map.
How many bridges and tunnels will you need?

Compare your route with a map showing the actual line from London to Bristol.
How close is your route?

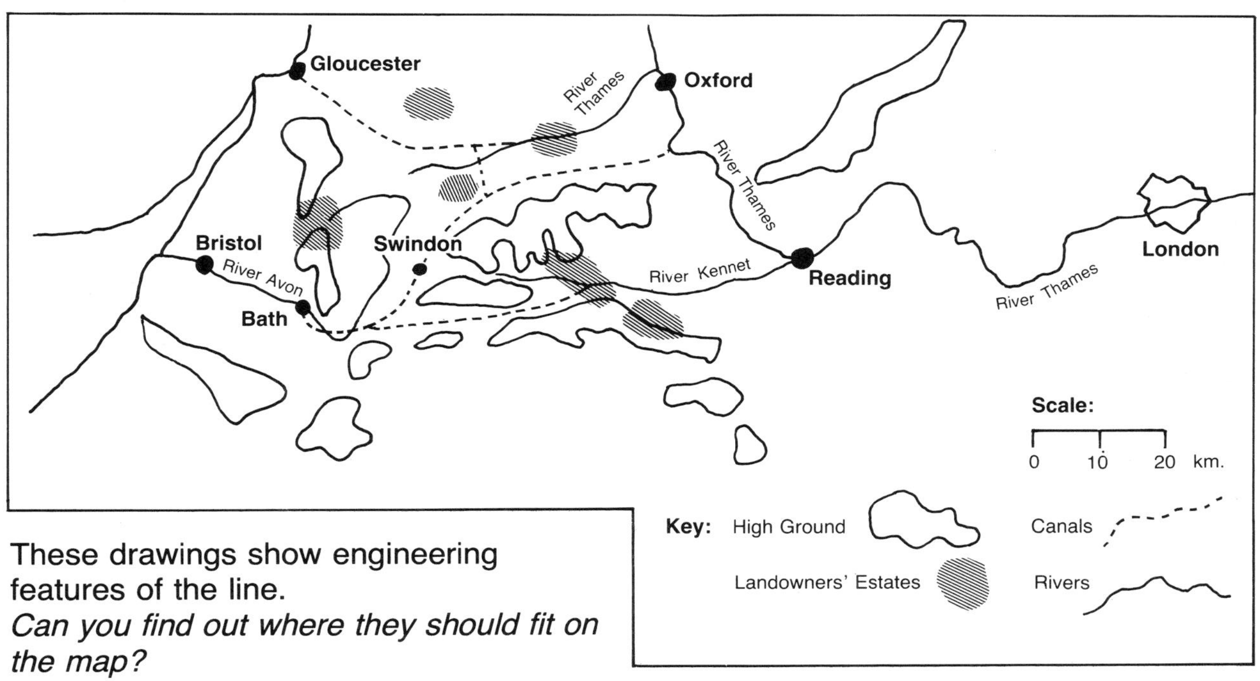

These drawings show engineering features of the line.
Can you find out where they should fit on the map?

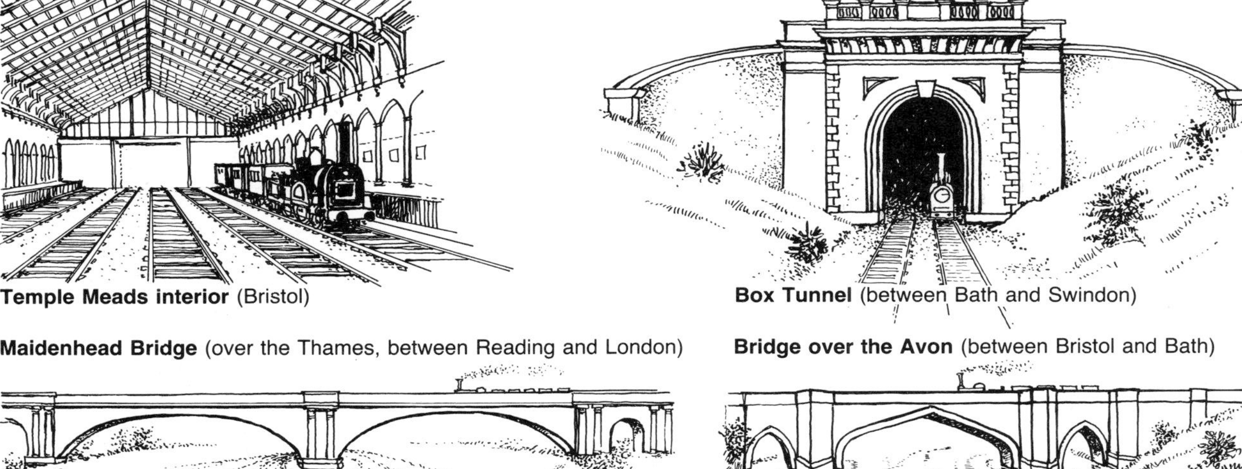

Temple Meads interior (Bristol)

Box Tunnel (between Bath and Swindon)

Maidenhead Bridge (over the Thames, between Reading and London)

Bridge over the Avon (between Bristol and Bath)

IN April 1846, London-based mail coaches were finally replaced by trains, which speeded the mail across land as steamships were to do on the packet routes. The quantity of mail being handled was increasing: the weekly average for letter deliveries in England and Wales was 2 970 598 in 1841; by 1847 it was 4 572 969.

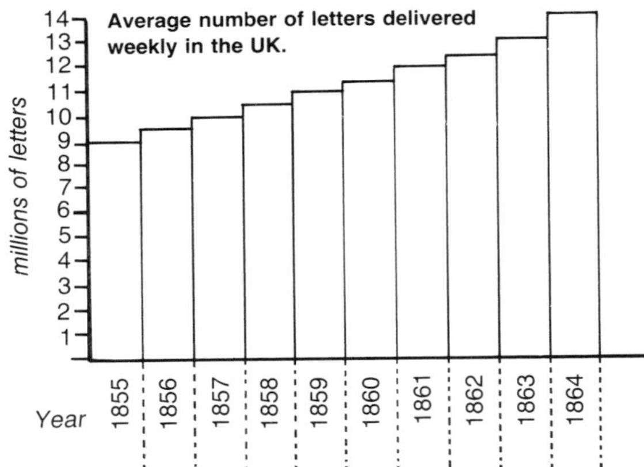

Travelling Post Offices on trains allowed the mail to be sorted en route and collected and distributed without stopping the train. The proposal for a standardised system of prepaid postage came from Rowland Hill in 1837. It was not introduced immediately, as may be seen by the 1839 petition.

It could still cost 8 d. to send a local letter in 1839 (average weekly wage 7 s.). A campaign led to the introduction of the penny post in 1840. The cost was 1 d. per ounce, regardless of distance. How does this compare with modern rates?

UNIFORM

Penny Postage

THE FOLLOWING

PETITION

TO THE

HOUSE OF COMMONS,

To Pass this Important Measure without delay,

Lies here for Signatures.

READER,

Sign the Petition without a moment's delay,

BECAUSE

IT MUST BE PRESENTED BEFORE FRIDAY NEXT, JULY THE 12TH.

To the Honourable the Commons in Parliament assembled.

The humble Petition of the undersigned Inhabitants of Westminster,

Sheweth,

THAT, an Englishman having invented the Uniform Penny Postage Plan, your Petitioners feel that the United Kingdom should not be behind France, and Belgium, and Prussia, and the United States, in getting it; they, therefore, humbly pray your Honourable House to give effect to the Uniform Penny Postage, payable in advance, *during the present Session of Parliament.*

And your Petitioners will ever pray.

PRINTED BY T. BRETTELL, RUPERT STREET, HAYMARKET.

THE work on sheet 17A will need **close supervision:** knives or scissors are sharp!

Local investigations

MARK on a map the position of all of the local post boxes. Are there any Victorian ones? Colour code them by age (date by monarch). Look at the base to check on the manufacturer. The Carron Works in Scotland made many of the boxes. (They also made the cannon, 'Carronades', that were aboard HMS *Victory*.) Can you track down any Carron boxes?

Investigate the distances between post boxes. What is the furthest distance any child might have to walk from home to post a letter?

Today's mail

Keep records of the time taken to deliver the school mail. Check the distance travelled. Work out the average journey times (a good maths project). Can you compare with Victorian delivery times?

Set up a postal service

Set up a Victorian Postal Service at Christmas. Make facsimile stamps with Victoria's head on (look at a stamp catalogue), seal the letters with wax (under supervision). Set up a Post Office in the corner with a high desk, quill pens, ink, and scales using pounds and ounces. A small panelled 'window' behind could show a winter scene.

Make a quill pen

A wing feather of any large bird will do. Goose is good. The feather can be hardened (cured) by boiling for a few minutes in water and drying (again for a few minutes) in the oven.

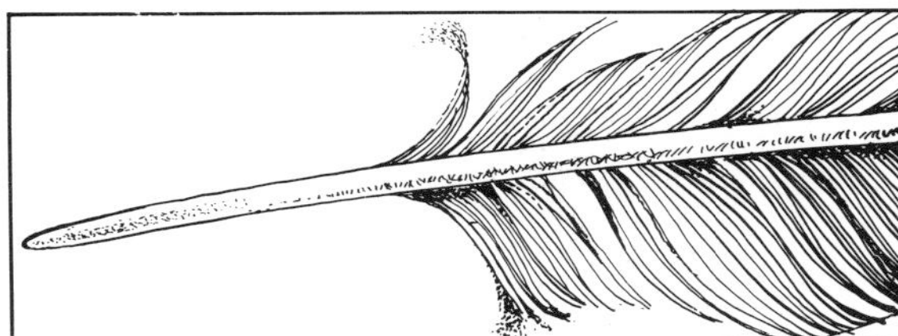

1 With the underside uppermost, make a long diagonal cut (about 2 cm) at the point.

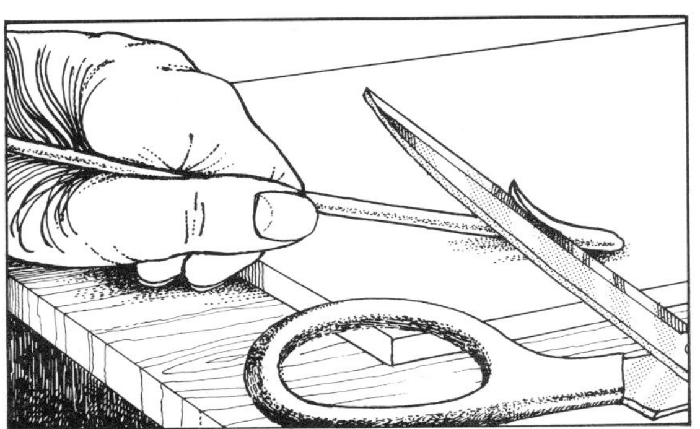

2 Trim the shoulders and cut off the point with scissors or a knife.

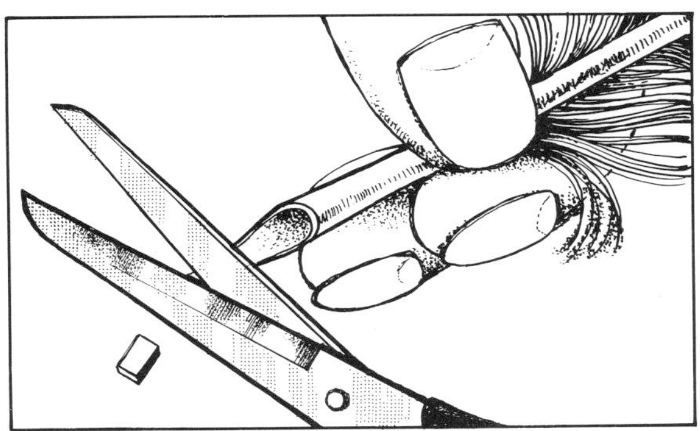

3 Pull out the internal membrane which is loose in the quill.

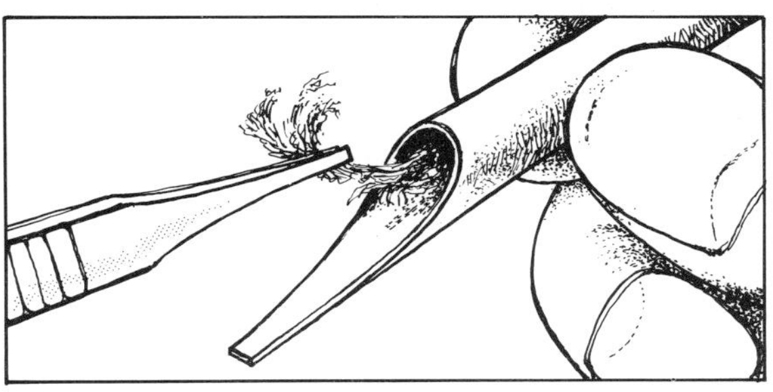

4 Holding the quill on a hard surface, make a slit at the end. If the quill has been hardened, squeezing will cause the slit to run further up the quill.

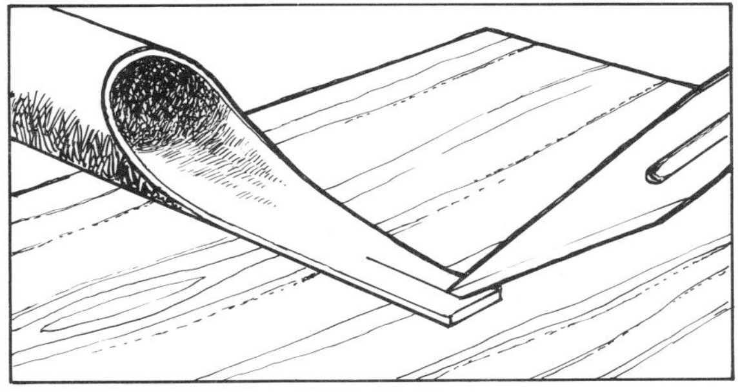

5 Finish with a slanted cut.

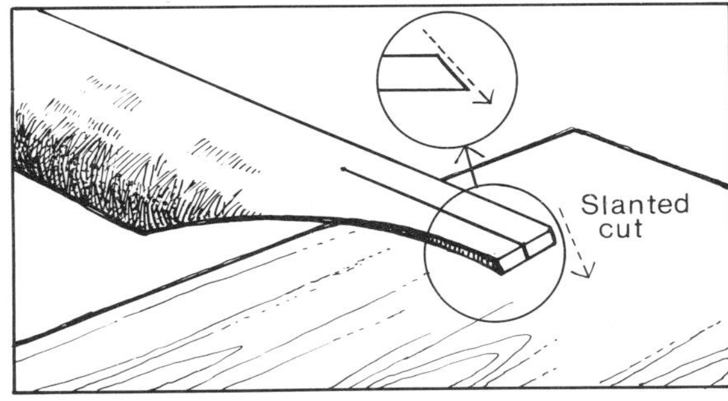

Cut away from you onto a hard board. **Take care!** Knives are sharp.

Write on a slope to prevent flooding and use non-waterproof ink which does not clog easily.

What is a 'pen-knife'?

The post

In this big box is the 'net' of an early post box.

First, cut out the big box and stick it on to card.

Next, colour the post box and cut it out.

Make up the model. Fold along all of the lines and glue the sides together.

Make your own 'net' of a modern post box. *How do the two boxes differ?*

How many different kinds of box can you find in your area?

This is a Victorian postman.
Cut round the figure roughly and stick it on to card.

Colour and cut out the postman.
Stand him beside the box.

Can you make a modern postman to go with your modern box?

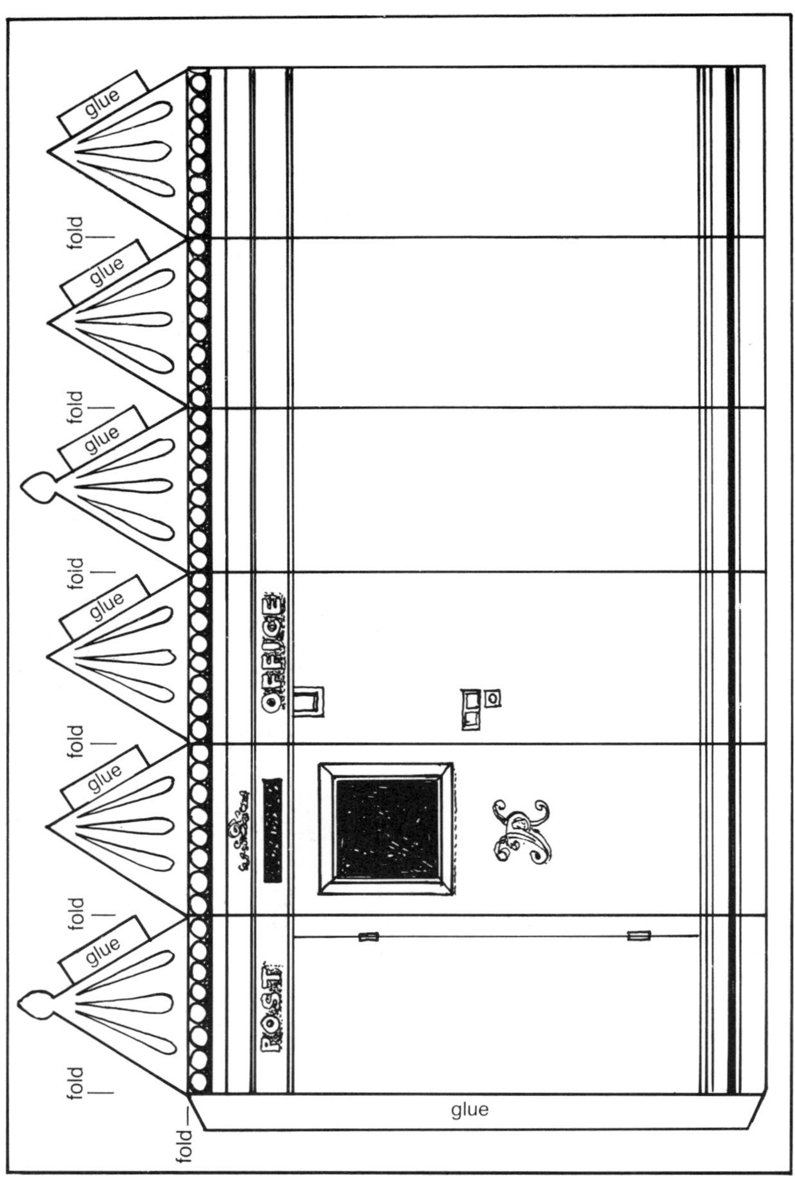

Many things were invented during Queen Victoria's reign. Not all were important or successful.

Work out what all of these are.
Can you say what has happened to them?

This vessel was the world's first powered

____

invented by the Rev. George Garrett

The world's first gummed

____

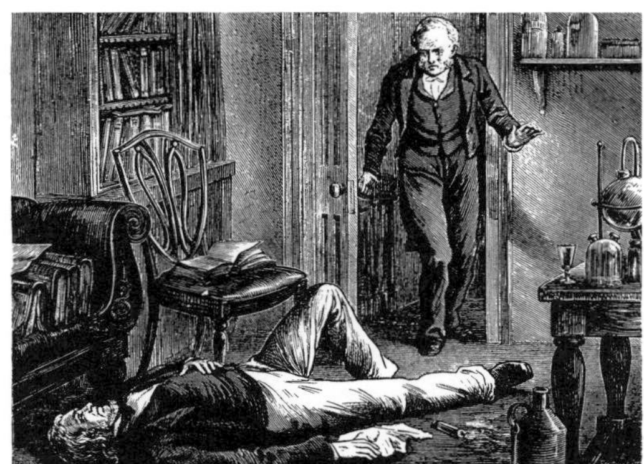

Dr James Simpson tried out

c________________ as an anaesthetic.

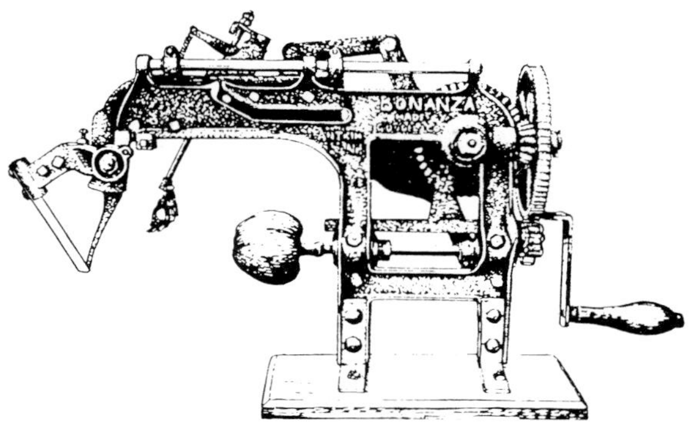

The amazing Bonanza

apple p________________ and

c________________

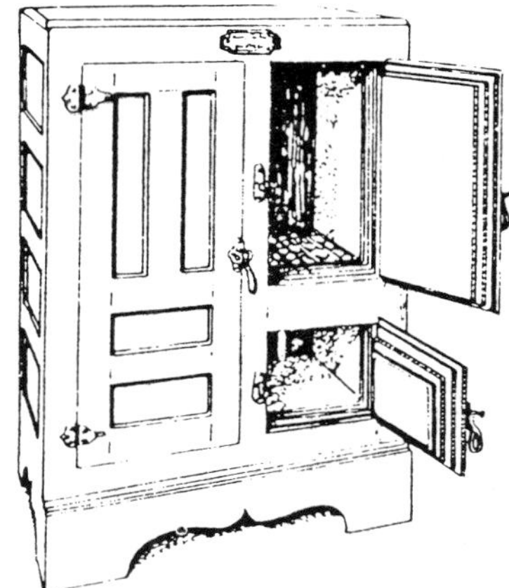

Blocks of ice in the cupboard (top right) kept food cool in the Seger's Dry Air

Syphon R________________

Early v________________

c________________ were so large that they had to be worked from a cart outside.

Christmas

MANY Victorian Christmas customs persist today so, with a little ingenuity, it is relatively easy to create a Victorian atmosphere in the classroom at Christmas time.

There was a nice mixture then of fervour and frivolity, with carol singers, bell ringing, spectacular pantomimes and circuses, rich food, trees, cards, and often elaborate present giving. Even Christmas day in the workhouse was not all bad.

'. . . a proper dinner was served in the large dining hall, looking bright and cheerful with mottoes, texts, designs and festoons. 470 men and women ate roast beef and plum pudding with coffee at the close . . . The diners disposed of 46 stones of beef, 6 of suet, 37 of potatoes, and the pudding contained 100 lb of plums, 50 lb of currants and 40 lb of sultanas. Sweets and tobacco came afterwards and entertainment was of a free and easy character.'

Leeds Workhouse 1860

Christmas food

READ out to the children the extract from Leeds Workhouse. How much food was consumed in metric measures? How much did each individual eat?

Sheet 19A shows the children how to make a Bible cake. You will need to use the Authorised Version of the Bible to decipher the recipe. (**a–l**: sugar, honey, butter, eggs, figs, almonds, raisons, leaven – baking powder, salt, spices, flour, milk.)

Decorations

Kissing under the mistletoe was a liberty much enjoyed by the Victorians. The opportunity was not to be rejected lightly.

He who will not when he may
When he will shall have nay.

Try to update the rhyme.

Make the classroom 'bright with mottoes, texts and festoons'. Make handmade evergreen decorations too.

Christmas cards

In 1880, the Post Office issued its first warning to post early for Christmas. Christmas cards were big business. Summerley's Home Treasury Office published the first pictorial card in 1846. It was designed by J.C. Horsley to an idea of Henry Coles. Find some early examples to copy.

Stocking fillers

An *apple* in the toe offers health and happiness.
An *orange* in the heel means a touch of luxury (oranges were very costly).
A new *penny* means prosperity.
A lump of rock *salt* brings good luck.
A piece of *coal* wrapped in tissue is a symbol of warmth in winter.
Plus a scrap book, crayons, a sugar mouse, marzipan wraps (date, fig or nut wrapped in marzipan).

How does this compare with a stocking today?

A Bible cake

The Christian religion was an important part of most people's lives in Victorian Britain. Knowledge of the Bible was taught at school.

This Victorian recipe shows off this knowledge. *Can you solve the puzzle and find the ingredients?* You will need a Bible.

a 225 g of Jeremiah chapter 6 verse 20

b One tablespoon of the first book of Samuel chapter 14 verse 25

c 225 g of Judges chapter 5 verse 25 (end)

d 3 of Jeremiah chapter 17 verse 11

e 225 g of chopped Nahum chapter 3 verse 12

f 50 g blanched and chopped Numbers chapter 17 verse 8

g 225 g of first book of Samuel chapter 30 verse 12

h A teaspoon of Amos chapter 4 verse 5

i A pinch of Leviticus chapter 2 verse 13

j Add second book of Chronicles chapter 9 verse 9 to taste

k 450 g of first book of Kings chapter 4 verse 22

l 3 tablespoons of Judges chapter 4 verse 19 (end)

(Note: leaven is baking powder)

Jeremiah, Samuel and the rest are books of the Bible. *In which part of the Bible are they found?*

What would the Victorians have used instead of grams?

INGREDIENTS			
a	____________	g	____________
b	____________	h	____________
c	____________	i	____________
d	____________	j	____________
e	____________	k	____________
f	____________	l	____________

Baking the cake

You will need the secret ingredients plus:

A large mixing bowl
20 cm round cake tin (deep)
Sieve for sifting
Greaseproof paper and a small quantity of margarine
Wire rack for cooling the cake
Mixing and measuring utensils

Beat the first three ingredients (**a,b,c**) in the mixing bowl until they turn into a soft, light-coloured, creamy mixture.

Add **d** one at a time, beating in well. You can now stir in **e, f** and **g.** Sift together **h, i, j,** and **k** before adding with **l**. Stir until well mixed.

Before you place the mixture in the cake tin, line the tin with greased greaseproof paper.

Bake at gas mark 3 or 160°C. The cake will take about 2 hours to cook properly. When it is cooked, turn it out on to the wire rack and leave it to cool.

A Christmas gift box

Cut out this shape on card. Colour in the decoration or stick on Victorian pictures from old cards or wrapping paper.

You can fill the container with sweets as a present or hang it on a Christmas tree.